Understanding Iran

Jerrold D. Green, Frederic Wehrey, Charles Wolf, Jr.

Prepared for the Smith Richardson Foundation

NATIONAL SECURITY RESEARCH DIVISION

The research described in this report was sponsored by the Smith Richardson Foundation and was conducted under the auspices of the International Security and Defense Policy Center within the RAND National Security Research Division (NSRD). NSRD conducts research and analysis for the Office of the Secretary of Defense, the Joint Staff, the Unified Commands, the defense agencies, the Department of the Navy, the Marine Corps, the U.S. Coast Guard, the U.S. Intelligence Community, allied foreign governments, and foundations.

Library of Congress Cataloging-in-Publication Data

Green, Jerrold D.
    Understanding Iran / Jerrold D. Green, Frederic Wehrey, Charles Wolf, Jr.
    p. cm.
    ISBN 978-0-8330-4558-4 (pbk. : alk. paper)
    1. Iran—Politics and government—1997– 2. Iran—Economic conditions—1997–
3. Iran—Foreign relations—1997– I. Wehrey, Frederic M. II. Wolf, Charles, 1924–
III. Rand Corporation. IV. Title.

    JQ1785.G74 2009
    320.955—dc22

                                                                2008035190

Published 2009 by the RAND Corporation
1776 Main Street, P.O. Box 2138, Santa Monica, CA 90407-2138
1200 South Hayes Street, Arlington, VA 22202-5050
4570 Fifth Avenue, Suite 600, Pittsburgh, PA 15213-2665
RAND URL: http://www.rand.org/
To order RAND documents or to obtain additional information, contact
Distribution Services: Telephone: (310) 451-7002;
Fax: (310) 451-6915; Email: order@rand.org

Preface

The United States has been working predominantly in the dark with respect to the Islamic Republic of Iran. All interested players, regardless of their political leanings or underlying motivations, suffer from America's collective ignorance about this uniquely complex country. This ignorance stems from Iran's denial of sustained physical access to American visitors, but it also stems from America's lack of access to and insight into the workings of the Iranian system itself, especially its economic system.

This gap is what the project reported on in this monograph addresses. The project's architects recognized that U.S. policymakers of all perspectives need to understand what motivates Iran and how it works. Fully aware of the analytic challenges that Iran offers, the project organizers turned to the Smith Richardson Foundation for assistance, with an eye to constructing a user-friendly and readable handbook that could enable U.S. policymakers to get up to speed on Iran in an efficient fashion.

This research was conducted within the International Security and Defense Policy Center (ISDP) of the RAND Corporation's National Security Research Division (NSRD). NSRD conducts research and analysis for the Office of the Secretary of Defense, the Joint Staff, the Unified Combatant Commands, the defense agencies, the Department of the Navy, the Marine Corps, the U.S. Coast Guard, the U.S. Intelligence Community, allied foreign governments, and foundations.

For more information on RAND's International Security and Defense Policy Center, contact the Director, James Dobbins. He can be reached by email at James_Dobbins@rand.org; by phone at 703-413-1100, extension 5134; or by mail at the RAND Corporation, 1200 S. Hayes Street, Arlington, VA 22202. More information about RAND is available at www.rand.org.

Contents

Figures and Tables

Figures

Tables

Summary

Over the years, there have been numerous efforts to locate the roots of the Islamic Republic's intentions and motivations in the distinctiveness of its political culture and history. A rich and ancient nation, Iran has always beguiled outsiders. This complexity, combined with America's lack of access to Iran since 1979, has produced a peculiar view of the Islamic Republic, a view defined by mystique and a superficial reading that places too much emphasis on Iran's "abnormal" and "exceptional" characteristics.

This document is a short, accessible guide intended to help U.S. policymakers understand the Islamic Republic. It offers a set of short analytic observations about the processes, institutions, networks, and actors that define Iran's politics, strategy, economic policy, and diplomacy. From these, it sets out an argument for appreciating the challenges and fundamentals of negotiating with Iran. The key findings can be summarized as follows:

• *Supreme Leader Ayatollah Ali Khamenei is Iran's most powerful figure, exerting "negative influence" and arbitrating over diverse actors and institutions.* Khamenei has often been overlooked as a weak and indecisive personality who occupies a powerful post but lacks charisma. Yet constitutionally and in practice, he remains Iran's ultimate political authority. Much of his formal power is exerted indirectly—through the appointment and oversight power he has with respect to Iran's quasi-democratic policy and legislative structures and its armed forces.

It is the informal realm, however, on which U.S. policymakers and analysts should focus most of their attention: The Leader exerts influence through his mediating role over contending factions, personal relationships with top military commanders, and the clerical representatives he has throughout Iran's key security institutions. Since the election of President Mahmoud Ahmadinejad in 2004, Khamenei's influence has grown—to a large extent because Ahmadinejad's radical posturing and increasing unpopularity enable Khamenei to appear more moderate and favorable by comparison.

Yet the Leader is not an omnipotent autocrat. The Iranian system contains numerous checks and balances on his power, resulting in a policy apparatus that can appear excessively ponderous to outsiders. The Leader's exercise of power is, moreover, bounded by his well-known preference for risk aversion and his desire to maintain the status quo.

• *Khamenei's sense of strategic confidence, distrust of the United States, and focus on Iranian sovereignty results in an aversion to compromise.* Some of Khamenei's status quo orientation can be attributed to his reading of Iran's recent gains in the wake of the U.S.-led invasion of Iraq, the 2006 Lebanon war, and other regional events. His speeches and writings evince a sense of strategic triumphalism—that is, the belief that if there is a "new Middle East," it is one that has tilted in favor of the Islamic Republic.

U.S. policymakers should be cognizant of how this outlook informs Khamenei's aversion to negotiations and compromise. The Leader harbors a deep-seated distrust of U.S. intentions—a sentiment that holds throughout Iran. Compromise, according to Khamenei, will only be seen as a sign of weakness, encouraging the United States to exert greater pressure on the Islamic Republic. For the Leader, justice, Islam, independence and self-sufficiency are paramount, and ultimately intertwined. For Iran to safeguard social justice and promote Islam, it must be politically independent; and it cannot be independent unless it is economically and technologically self-sufficient—hence the importance of an indigenous nuclear fuel cycle.

• *The Islamic Revolutionary Guards Corps (IRGC) exerts significant influence over Iran's politics and economy, much of it occurring at an informal level among networks of IRGC ex-commanders and veterans.*

Among the constituencies over which the Leader presides, the IRGC has emerged as the country's most powerful. The IRGC's estimated 120,000 active-duty personnel fulfill a number of functions related to internal security, external defense and power projection, and regime survival.

Yet it is in the informal realm where the IRGC's presence has been most visible, via a network of ex-commanders and veterans who have ascended to powerful posts in the Cabinet, the legislature, the media, education, and the business sectors. While it is important not to overstate the ideological uniformity or coordination among these individuals, there is a marked sense of common identity and outlook that is broadly technocratic, authoritarian, and populist.

• *IRGC networks control key sectors of Iran's market, a development that could presage increasing factional debates between economically oriented pragmatists and more-dogmatic currents.* The IRGC brings significant financial resources to its political power, controlling an array of subsidiary companies that have penetrated virtually every sector of the Iranian market—from construction and real estate to laser eye surgery and automobile manufacturing. Reportedly, the IRGC also operates illicit smuggling networks that constitute a vast shadow economy.

The IRGC's business ascendancy has been secured through no-bid contracts and occasional strong-arm tactics, such as the IRGC's closure of the newly opened Imam Khomeini International Airport in 2004, reportedly to eject a Turkish contractor that had won a bid on airport operations from an IRGC firm. This has provoked nascent dissent from displaced business elites, who view the IRGC as a mere substitute for the clerical oligarchs.

Despite the IRGC's self-enrichment and political domination, U.S. policymakers and analysts should avoid demonizing the institution as a monolithic whole. Debates and fissures have surfaced among the IRGC veterans on the same subjects that define the broader Iranian political spectrum: reconciling modernization with Islamic legitimacy and, especially, the opportunity costs associated with Iran's defiance on the nuclear program. Pragmatic currents in the IRGC could emerge as an increasingly powerful force.

• *Iran's oil-dominated economy exhibits unique pathologies, some of them related to the bureaucratic disarray and political interference that afflict economic policymaking.* Understanding the dynamics of Iran's oil economy is especially critical for understanding Iran's political processes and gauging regime stability: The availability of revenues may affect the speed of decisionmaking, and greater wealth liquidity enables the regime to manage potential dissent on unpopular policies. Iran's oil exports are large, totaling $60 billion in 2007 and making up 35 percent of the gross domestic product (GDP). Yet Iran is hindered from fully harnessing this wealth by the so-called Dutch disease, which is the impairment of a balanced, multi-sector economy because of the surfeit of a scarce resource that commands large rents from the rest of the world and impedes development of other sectors of the economy.

This condition is compounded by excessive political interference in the economy, illustrated most starkly by President Ahmadinejad's raiding of the Oil Stabilization Fund to provide subsidies in lieu of carrying out structural reform. Moreover, the regime has largely failed in its efforts to attract foreign direct investment (FDI); foreign capital is deterred by flip-flop policies and lack of coordination among the roughly dozen government bodies that are mobilized in economic decisionmaking.

For the Iranian citizenry, the aftershocks of this mismanagement are felt in widespread fuel rationing, electricity blackouts, and skyrocketing inflation, all of which have provoked a growing backlash against Ahmadinejad. The middle class in Tehran is being hit especially hard, particularly on housing. Yet public awareness of links between these hardships and the regime's expenditures on the nuclear program or the IRGC's illicit activities remains limited and fragmentary. Although the economy remains vulnerable to sudden shocks, such as the disruption of oil through the Strait of Hormuz, it appears more durable for the short term than is commonly assumed. Public forbearance of the regime's economic mismanagement is nurtured by a degree of oil-generated prosperity.

• *Iran's factionalized elite operates in three overlapping clusters, the fluidity and dynamism of which militate against the United States placing its hopes on one particular cluster.* The political factions in contention over the Iranian economy and other aspects of the state remain the key to understanding the deeper processes of the Islamic Republic. It is possible to generalize the factions as three overlapping and highly fluid currents, or "clusters," that transcend formal policy institutions, cut across class and social barriers, and have shaped Iranian politics since 1979: conservatives, reformists and pragmatists. All three clusters agree that it is necessary to preserve the Islamic Republic, protect Iranian sovereignty, and extend Iran's influence. The differences emerge over how to do this, whether and how civil society and pluralism can be reconciled with fidelity to the Revolution, and Iran's integration with the world.

The current axis of contention is between the conservatives, especially those who have refashioned themselves as "principlists," and the "pragmatists," who are embodied in Ali Akbar Rafsanjani. Splits have also emerged among the principlists and the conservatives over Ahmadinejad's handling of the economy, the nuclear program, Iran's policy in Iraq, and other issues. The reformists, meanwhile, remain a spent force and are working to rebuild their constituency and reorganize their political machinery. The most significant obstacle they face is that their efforts at rapprochement with the United States under former President Khatami produced nothing—a fact that has been highlighted repeatedly by hard-liners. The pragmatists, for their part, are frequently attacked as "opportunists" by their more dogmatic opponents.

What this somewhat abridged spectrum reveals is the fluidity and complexity of the Iranian environment and the inadvisability of trying to social engineer factional change. Moreover, no single faction lines up neatly with U.S. interests across the spectrum; for example, a social progressive might still see the necessity of supporting Lebanese Hizballah.

• *Iran's nuclear ambitions are stoked by factional struggles and bureaucratic interests, making the issue less sensitive to external pressure than is commonly recognized.* Iran's nuclear program—and particularly its retention of an indigenous fuel cycle—has attained a symbolic resonance comparable to then–Prime Minister Mohammad Mossadegh's nationalization of Iranian oil in 1951. In both cases, energy resources encapsulate nationalist themes of modernity, sovereignty, self-sufficiency, and non-submission to Western control.

Each faction has used the nuclear program for political purposes, attempting to garner support from key constituencies and frequently invoking public opinion—as a reason for pursuing the program regardless of pressure (the hard-liners) or as a factor for caution (the pragmatists). While most Iranians agree on Iran's right to unrestrictedly seek modern technologies, consensus clearly fades over the price Iranians are willing to pay for program continuation in terms of sanctions, loss of confidence in investment, capital flight, and estrangement from the international community.

Aside from the broader public, there are other important constituencies and "audiences" in the nuclear arena. The strongest supporters of Iran's nuclear drive are those that stand to lose the most from its termination. Foremost among these is Iran's Atomic Energy Organization (AEO), which oversees the program's scientific and technical dimensions. Another is the IRGC, which provides security for all nuclear-related installations and, given its current role as custodian of Iran's ballistic missile arsenal, would likely exert command and control over any nuclear weapons.

U.S. policymakers should understand how these domestic political factors have lent the nuclear program its own momentum, making it less susceptible to international pressure than might be expected.

• *The nonsectarian appeal to Arab public opinion that Iran has incorporated in its dealings with the rest of the Arab world has affected Arab support for U.S. policies in the region.* Iran has long pursued a policy of "hyper-activism" on pan-Arab issues, appealing to Arab public opinion to outmaneuver and embarrass U.S.-allied Arab regimes and to break out of its fundamental cultural isolation from the larger Middle East—what one commentator termed the "Shiite ghetto." This dynamic has grown more pronounced under Ahmadinejad, as illustrated by his posturing on the nuclear issue and his brazen denial of the Holocaust, which was calculated to embarrass and upstage traditional patrons of the Palestinian cause, such as the al-Saud.

Yet Arab public opinion remains a fickle resource for Tehran, subject to rapid swings, often caused by Iranian policies or missteps. Any

Arab applause that Iran garners for supporting Hizballah or defying U.S. pressure on the nuclear issue is undermined by its policies in Iraq. Even inside Iran, the appeal to the Arab publics, or "Arab street strategy," has attracted critics, causing Tehran to make a more pronounced effort to engage with its Arab neighbors.

In attempting to build Arab consensus against Iran, U.S. policymakers should be mindful of how public opinion on Iran affects the calculus of Arab regimes. Arab rulers have long recognized that Iran can play the trump card of rejectionism and defiance of the West, which can be extremely appealing to disgruntled Arab publics. Moreover, the United States should recognize that Arab distrust of Iran does not equal de facto support for U.S. policies: Opinion polls frequently show that Iran and the United States are viewed with equal suspicion.

• *The United States must overcome the mystique of talking with Iran while managing its expectations and being mindful of unique Iranian negotiating attributes.* The U.S. approach to Iran is defined by a peculiar form of mystique that defies America's history of engaging other international actors of varying shades of enmity (for example, North Korea, Serbs, and Somali warlords). This aversion to talking to Iran has squandered several opportunities to reduce tension—in 2001, on the margins of the Bonn talks on Afghanistan, and in 2003, on the eve of the 2003 invasion of Iraq. In these cases, Iran came to the table because of gratitude and fear, two motives that are largely absent today, replaced by a strategic confidence and the perception of diminished U.S. credibility and maneuverability.

There is value in negotiating with Iran, even if the likelihood for a breakthrough is distant. First, negotiations broaden U.S. contacts inside the regime and produce more information about its processes, both of which might generate unexpected openings for influence later. Second, negotiations reduce misunderstandings that can escalate into conflict. Third, negotiations can help de-mystify the Islamic Republic, reducing the U.S. tendency to treat it as an exceptional and abnormal actor in the international system.

U.S. policymakers should be mindful that while there is nothing especially risky or exotic about talking with Iran, Iranians have specific, unique negotiating attributes. First and foremost is their pronounced sense of victimization. Japanese and European negotiators have long noted that Iranians must feel as if they "earned" any concessions to their demands. There is also a tendency to defer the resolution of weighty issues, to avoid incrementalism, and to revisit issues that both sides previously agreed were closed. Others have emphasized the Iranian willingness to maximize short-term gains to the detriment of long-term strategic advantage. Underpinning all of these attributes is the deeply embedded Persian cultural convention of ta'arof—a display of exaggerated politeness, deference, and self-deprecation—that has simultaneously enchanted and exasperated Western negotiators.

Acknowledgments

We would like to thank Dr. Marin Strmecki of the Smith Richardson Foundation for encouraging us to proceed with and helping us formulate the idea for this project. We would also like to thank Ms. Judy Bearer at RAND for her diligent assistance and patience in assembling the various components of this report and for helping us bring this project to a successful conclusion.

Abbreviations

AAC	Assembly of Assertive Clerics
AEO	Atomic Energy Organization
BIC	Board of Islamic Coalition
CBI	Central Bank of Iran
CIA	Central Intelligence Agency (U.S.)
CPI	consumer price index
EU	European Union
FDI	foreign direct investment
FIPPA	Foreign Investment Promotion and Protection Act
FTZ	free trade zone
FYDP	five-year development plan
GC	Guardian Council
GCC	Gulf Cooperation Council
GDP	gross domestic product
GNI	gross national income
IISS	International Institute for Strategic Studies
IMF	International Monetary Fund
IPO	initial public offering
IRGC	Islamic Revolutionary Guards Corps
IRI	Islamic Republic of Iran
IRIB	Islamic Republic of Iran Broadcasting Corporation

IRNA	Islamic Republic News Agency
IRP	Islamic Republican Party
ISDP	International Security and Defense Policy Center
LAPFI	Law on Attraction and Promotion of Foreign Investment
LEF	Law Enforcement Forces
M2	money supply
NBR	National Bureau of Asian Research
NIE	National Intelligence Estimate
NITA	National Iranian Tax Administration
NPT	Treaty on the Nonproliferation of Nuclear Weapons (informally known as the Nuclear NonProliferation Treaty)
NSC	National Security Council
NSRD	National Security Research Division
OECD	Organisation for Economic Co-operation and Development
OIC	Organization of the Islamic Conference
OIETAI	Organization for Investment, Economic and Technical Assistance of Iran
OSC	Open Source Center
OSF	Oil Stabilization Fund
POI	Iranian Privatization Organization
PRGS	Pardee RAND Graduate School
SAC	Society of Assertive Clerics
SIS	Society of Instructors of the Seminaries
SME	Society of Muslim Engineers
SNSC	Supreme National Security Council
UAE	United Arab Emirates
UN	United Nations

UNSC	United Nations Security Council
USIP	United States Institute for Peace
USSR	Union of Soviet Socialist Republics
WTO	World Trade Organization

CHAPTER ONE

Introduction

Birth of the Project

The genesis of this guidebook can be traced to a seeming paradox: The more that political actors and observers in the United States talk about the Islamic Republic of Iran, the more apparent it becomes that little is known about this uniquely complex polity. And this lack of knowledge transcends partisan and ideological boundaries—all interested players, regardless of their political leanings or underlying motivations, suffer from America's collective ignorance about Iran. In part we can attribute this lack of knowledge to the fact that most Americans are denied sustained access to Iran. So, too, can we attribute it to the no less important fact that the Iranian system is cumbersome, unwieldy, complex, and hard to understand—all of which constitute an attribute, not a flaw, of the system's design. The Iranian system is intensely driven by personality and, at the same time, subsumes very weighty institutions, both formal elements of the state and equally important non-state actors. Physical access to Iran is thus only one key essential for understanding it. The other essential key is access to and insight into the workings of the system itself.

An additional component of the paradox is the Iranian economic system. Despite its historical clout and current decay, the Iranian economy is in equally large measures both important and ignored, and thus misunderstood. It tends to be referred to far more often than it undergoes systematic analysis. The resultant lacuna is what this project was meant to address; the project's architects recognized the importance of the Islamic Republic of Iran and the need to know about it. U.S.

policymakers of all perspectives need to understand what motivates Iran and how it works. Fully aware of the analytic challenges that Iran offers, the project organizers turned to the Smith Richardson Foundation for assistance, with an eye to constructing a user-friendly and readable handbook that would enable American policymakers to get up to speed on Iran in an efficient fashion.

Background

In canvassing a range of global threats, the National Security Council's 2006 *National Security Strategy* warned, "We may face no greater challenge from a single country than from Iran." Adding to this, President George W. Bush stated in 2007 that Tehran's pursuit of nuclear energy risked starting World War III. Yet despite the severity of these pronouncements, Iran remains among the most poorly understood countries in the world and, for most Americans, terra incognita. A small community of American analysts in the government, academia, and the country's think tanks is, of course, working on Iran, but the overwhelming majority of them have never been to Iran or have visited only briefly. The consequences of this unfamiliarity have been distinctly negative for American policy, pushing most analyses toward a highly reductionist view. We thus believe there is a critical need for both a fresh look at Iran and a policy-relevant "handbook" that synthesizes the existing analyses and, most important, draws from non-American experts who can offer a different interpretive lens for viewing this seemingly opaque system.

With this in mind, we convened a two-day conference of analysts and observers of the Islamic Republic of Iran in late October 2007 in Rome, Italy. We chose the participants from a pool of experts whose names may not be immediately familiar to Washington-based policymakers. This strategy was by design; it reflects our conviction that the best insights on Iran frequently come from non-Americans who meet three broad criteria: They have uncommon access to Iran, they have Persian language capabilities, and they have a depth of experience dealing with Iranians from a broad political and societal spectrum. At the same time, we chose to balance these perspectives by considering the exigencies of U.S. policymaking: The RAND team included a former U.S. ambassador and career Foreign Service officer, a long-time consultant to the Central Intelligence Agency (CIA), and a former Joint Staff analyst. All of our guest scholars were asked to distill their insights on specific aspects of the Iranian system in short papers that we distributed to attendees prior to the workshop. Our meeting, held in a congenial setting, free from the pressures of Washington, produced a series of rich conversations among expert observers of Iran whom we regard as some of the world's best informed.

Contents of This Document

This monograph presents the fruit of our workshop discussions in the form of a detailed and insightful, yet compact and user-friendly guide to the Islamic Republic of Iran. Chapter Two explores in separate sections five specific features of the Iranian system: political landscape, the economy, leadership and political decisionmaking, approach to Arab neighbors, and negotiating style. Chapter Three presents our conclusions. Appendixes A, B, and C, contain, respectively, the workshop agenda, the papers written by the attendees, and the attendees' biographies.

Features of the Iranian System

In this chapter, we explore the Iranian system, concentrating on the following features:

- *The political landscape.* We look at the key institutions of the political elite, focusing particularly on the important role of Supreme Leader Ayatollah Ali Khamenei as a mediator of Iran's policy disputes and the growing domestic primacy of the Islamic Revolutionary Guards Corps (IRGC).
- *The economy.* The subjects here are Iran's oil-dependent economy and its attendant pathologies; the sensitivity of Iran's gross domestic product (GDP) to fluctuations in world oil prices and the value of Iran's oil exports; the myriad government entities involved in economic policy formulation and execution; the correlation of wealth distribution with political influence among elite actors.
- *Leadership and political decisionmaking.* We look at factionalism as a determinant of Iranian political behavior; dogmatism and opportunism in Iranian political culture; deference and indifference to public opinion among the elite; the importance of collective action and consensus in a multipolar decisionmaking structure. Iran's nuclear program is used as a case study to observe these processes at work.
- *Approach to Arab neighbors.* The topics here are Iran's influence and resonance among Arab publics and regimes; Iran's "Arab street strategy" as a driver for Iranian brinksmanship and assertiveness; the risks and benefits of employing Arab regimes as America's interlocutors and allies against the Islamic Republic.

- *Negotiating style.* This entails determining whether there is a uniquely Iranian style of deal-making; navigation of Iran's labyrinthine business culture and lessons for U.S. strategy; discerning cultural asymmetries in Iranian and U.S. approaches to negotiation—what one participant termed, "playing poker with chess-players."

Iran's Political Landscape: Individuals and Institutions

At its core, the Iranian system is closed, secretive, informal, and clannish—descriptors more aptly applied to a conspiratorial cabal than to a "normal" regime. The system is also intensely fractured and multipolar, in some cases by accident, in others by bureaucratic design. Taken in sum, these characteristics suggest a gridlocked political system, a tendency to lurch from crisis to crisis, and an overall drift toward strategic incoherence. Yet this observation is only partially accurate. Iran *does* function, often with remarkable cleverness, perspicacity, and adroitness on the diplomatic front. A preference for consensus and collective action, mediation by the Supreme Leader, and the elite's invocation of public opinion provide the "lubricant" for Iran's complex policy apparatus, enabling contending factions to close ranks. Often, decisiveness among the political elite is *issue dependent*; for example, there is greater agreement on relations with the United States and the nuclear program than on Iran's relations with the Arab world. Throughout its history, the Iranian system has shown the ability, when necessary, to affect drastic reversals in long-held paradigms, two notable examples being the "poisoned chalice" of the Iran-Iraq truce and the opening of relations with Saudi Arabia.

To understand these complex processes, one must have a basic understanding of the major players and formal institutions in the Iranian system. And one must start with the Supreme Leader, Ayatollah Khamenei. As Iran's most powerful political figure, his vision of the Islamic Republic has remained remarkably resolute and consistent over the past 18 years.

The Supreme Leader: Influence and Worldview

Ayatollah Ali Khamenei has frequently been overlooked or outright dismissed as a weak and indecisive personality who occupies a powerful post but lacks charisma. Much of this interpretation stems principally from the controversy surrounding his succession as Supreme Leader following Ayatollah Rohullah Khomeini's death in 1989 and from his clerical credentials, which are lackluster compared with those of other figures.[1] Despite these drawbacks, however, he has long exercised influence over the Iranian system through "negative power"—for example, not necessarily by formulating original policy, but by blocking alternative approaches. Much of his strength rests on his presumed moral authority and his skillful orchestration of informal networks, as well as recent shifts in the international and domestic context. For instance, the sense of embattlement that has developed among the body politic because of increased international pressure on Iran has enabled Khamenei to bolster the revolution's sagging legitimacy and discredit any moves toward reform as externally inspired. Along the same lines, he appears adroit at playing a "good-cop/bad-cop" role in Iranian factional politics, as he did when he publicly criticized the Guardian Council (GC) for disqualifying reformist parliamentary candidates in 2004, despite the fact that he ultimately has responsibility for appointing GC members. This public distancing of himself from the GC's decisionmaking was likely a deliberate tactic to portray himself as more democratic by comparison.

Since 2004, Khamenei has seen his influence expand. He exerts informal control over the elected conservative parliament through its speaker, Gholam Ali Haddad-Adel, whose daughter is married to Khamenei's son. He also enjoys support from the IRGC, whose top leadership he appoints and whose role in Iranian political life has grown considerably in recent years.[2] His principal rival in the Iranian system,

---

[1]   For an overview of these disputes and Khamenei's meager clerical standing, see Geiling, 1997. For a recent analysis of the Supreme Leader's worldview, see Sadjadpour, 2008.

[2]   The Supreme Leader's authority within the IRGC may have limits. His relations with former IRGC commander Mohsen Rezai were reported to be contentious, stemming from Rezai's effective upstaging of Khamenei's authority during the Iran-Iraq war.

former President Akbar Hashemi Rafsanjani, has been discredited by rampant perceptions of corruption and nepotism. The Supreme Leader has also benefited from the disenchantment of Iran's youth, who largely disengaged themselves from political activism when the expectations of the Khatami era went unmet.[3] Finally, the 2005 election of President Mahmoud Ahmadinejad, a radical and increasingly unpopular Iranian figure, has been a further boon to Khamenei's power. The public and factional backlash against Ahmadinejad has reinforced Khamenei's role as an arbiter and made him appear comparatively more moderate and popular.

In domestic policy preferences, the Supreme Leader leans toward the status quo, being fairly pragmatic in his drive for self-survival but defaulting toward a more hard-line ideological stance. Put differently, Khamenei mediates between the competing themes of republicanism and theocracy in the Islamic Republic, aware that an excessive drift toward the first of these would effectively obviate the position of Supreme Leader. On international issues, he has been markedly risk averse, preferring neither confrontation nor accommodation. He has been paralyzed by mistrust toward the United States, interpreting U.S. actions as pretexts for eroding the republic's revolutionary foundations through either gradual dissolution (as occurred in the Union of Soviet Socialist Republics [USSR]) or abrupt democratic change spurred by civil society (i.e., a "velvet revolution"). U.S. intentions, he has stated in his speeches, are ultimately geared toward reestablishing the patron-client relationship that existed under the Shah. Accordingly, Khamenei believes that any Iranian moves toward compromise will be seen as a sign of weakness and will encourage the United States to exert even greater pressure.

This aversion to compromise has been strengthened by the triumphalism that Khamenei brings to his reading of regional events—the belief that since the fall of Iraq's Saddam Husayn, and especially since the summer 2006 Lebanon war, the tide of history favors the Islamic Republic. Parodying U.S. rhetoric, Khamenei has argued that recent

---

[3]   President Mohammad Khatami, a reformist, served two terms, from August 1997 to August 2005. He was replaced by the ultra-conservative Ahmadinejad.

years have indeed seen the "birth pangs of a new Middle East," but in his case, the new Middle East is increasingly sympathetic toward Iran. Khamenei likely believes that much of this popular acclaim rests on the Islamic Republic's resolute animosity to Israel, which he, like policymakers in Washington, has viewed as a critical impediment to U.S.-Iranian relations. Despite the fact that anti-Israeli rhetoric has little meaning for the Iranian public and that key Iranian leaders have shown a willingness to barter this hostility for better relations with the United States, Khamenei has remained steadfast in his contempt.

In addition to Khamenei's paranoia about U.S. intentions and opposition to Israel, four other themes appear to shape his worldview. These themes, distilled from an extensive survey of his speeches in the past 10 years, are justice, Islam, independence, and self-sufficiency. For Iran to safeguard social justice and promote Islam, Khamenei has stated, Iran must be politically independent, a condition that hinges on economic and technological self-sufficiency. His speeches also evince the nuclear issue's almost mythic significance in linking these four themes. Despite evidence to the contrary, Khamenei has repeatedly pointed to the domestic economic benefits of retaining the full enrichment cycle, seeing in it a solution for Iran's "scientific retardation" and a sine qua non for Iran's political sovereignty. Given this fixation, Khamenei is unlikely to allow the relinquishment of an indigenous fuel cycle, which is viewed as Iran's "national right."

Taken in sum, these features of the Supreme Leader's worldview have important implications for U.S. policy. At age 70, the Supreme Leader most likely cannot effect a drastic reinvention of the "Death to America" culture that has nourished his thinking. Any policy action that forces him to back down publicly is clearly a non-starter, and back-channel overtures may be similarly dismissed—as long as he perceives the United States as unable to present a credible threat to the Republic's survival. Former Russian Foreign Minister Sergey Lavrov's visit to Iran provides one recent indication of this "strategic confidence": Lavrov reportedly endured an hours-long lecture from the Supreme Leader, returning empty handed and "disgusted."

One potential venue for reaching the Supreme Leader is his closest advisors, who include Ayatollahs Safi Golpayegani and Mohammad Reza Mahdavi Kani, as well as former foreign ministers such as Ali Akbar Velayati and Kamal Kharrazi. Another, formal venue is the Strategic Council on Foreign Relations—an advisory body he created in June 2006 as a "shadow cabinet" to provide sinecure for Khatami-era officials. The Council reportedly induced the Supreme Leader to release the 15 British sailors and marines seized by IRGC naval forces from the H.M.S. *Cornwall* in March 2007. It is important to note, however, that for the Supreme Leader, the consensus of other elites does not imply their equal *involvement* as much as their equal *implication*. Consensus is best thought of as a "safety net" for the Supreme Leader, one that absolves him of ultimate culpability for any policy that goes awry. Once a decision has been made, the elite are all responsible for it, with little room for opting out or exploiting mistakes or setbacks. In addition, consensus, however illusory, is an insurance policy against foreign exploitation of internal differences.

The National Security Establishment and the Rise of the Revolutionary Guards

Much of the Supreme Leader's influence rests on his ability to mediate, co-opt, and placate constituencies within Iran's defense and security establishment. Figure 2.1 is a rough schematic of these major institutions and their formal lines of authority.

Major national security issues are decided in the Supreme National Security Council (SNSC), which comprises the president, the defense and foreign ministers, the commander of the IRGC, and several appointees, or "representatives," of the Supreme Guide. The SNSC is broadly reflective of the elite, and its secretary (Saeed Jalili,[4] who replaced Ali Larijani in October 2007) is, broadly speaking, the equivalent of the U.S. National Security Adviser.

---

[4] Jalili's background is important. A former Basiji veteran of the Iran-Iraq war, he served as a professor of international relations and, beginning in 1989, a civil servant in the Foreign Ministry before becoming SNSC secretary. In his books and other writings, he has called for a "principled" foreign policy that adheres closely to the Iranian revolution's Islamist ideals—views that place him squarely in the Jihadi/conservative cluster of President Ahmadinejad. (*BBC Monitoring*, 2007a)

Figure 2.1
Major Institutions of the Iranian Defense Establishment

RAND *MG771-2.1*

The most important point to notice about the SNSC structure is that the president, Ahmadinejad, wields little authority in matters of defense despite his chairmanship of the Council and his headline-grabbing bravado. As noted earlier, it is the Supreme Leader who wields constitutional authority as commander-in-chief and (perhaps more important) exercises vast influence through his mediating role, his personal relationships with top commanders, and the presence of his clerical representatives throughout the security institutions. The Supreme Leader has special representatives in the SNSC (Hasan Rowhani); he also has special advisers for foreign affairs (former Foreign Minister Akbar Velayati) and military affairs (former IRGC Commander Yahya

Rahim Safavi). Khamenei is likely to consult these former officials and others when they do not participate in important sessions of the SNSC.

Foremost among the security institutions is Iran's powerful IRGC (Sepah-e Pasdaran-e Enghelab-e Islami). This group's growing politicization and increasing involvement in Iran's economic sphere—starting in 1997 but reaching its full apogee in 2004—can arguably be termed Iran's "third revolution." The IRGC's estimated 120,000 personnel carry out a number of functions related to internal security, external defense, and regime survival, and the IRGC fields an army, a navy, and an air force. In line with the IRGC's original charter of defending the revolution, it has installations in all of Iran's major cities that are organized into quick reaction groups to serve as a reserve against unrest. In rural regions, the IRGC operates with other security forces in various missions, including border control, counter-narcotics, and disaster relief. The IRGC has primacy over Iranian unconventional warfare options; it maintains tight control over the development and deployment of Iran's ballistic missiles and wields an external terrorism capability through its elite, Qods force. Were Iran to develop and field nuclear weapons, the IRGC would likely oversee their storage, training, and deployment infrastructure.

Yet the IRGC's growing primacy in Iranian political and economic life may far outstrip its actual military significance. It is important to understand that the political and economic weight of the IRGC veterans' influence does not derive merely from their service in the corps. Instead, it is their service in the Iran-Iraq war—membership in the same unit, participation in the same battle, a link with a particular commander. That commonality provides them with a shared outlook and a network that carries over into politics, economic activity, and society.

Beginning with the IRGC's episodic confrontations against reform activists during the Khatami era, the IRGC took on an increasingly political role, one that enabled it, by design or by accident, to emerge as a sort of "praetorian guard" for conservatives seeking to remove Khatami supporters from political power. In 2003, former members of the IRGC or its associates took control of numerous city and town councils, paving the way for their entry into legislative politics during the 2004 parliamentary elections. Ninety-one of 152 new members elected to the Majles (the Islamic Consultative Assembly) in February 2004 had a background in the Guards, and 34 former Guards officers now hold senior-level posts in the government. In the 2005 presidential election, Ahmadinejad was one of four candidates from the Guards. Influential figures such as Ali Larijani (replaced as secretary of the SCNS in late 2007), Ezzatolah Zarghami (head of the Islamic Republic of Iran Broadcasting Corporation [IRIB]), and Mohsen Rezai (secretary of the Expediency Council), and assorted heads of economic foundations, or bonyads, are part of the Guard generation. Finally, there are robust intellectual resources behind these personal networks; the IRGC administers two universities, two think tanks, and assorted policy journals and media outlets.

Moreover, the IRGC oversees or owns important interests in the oil, construction, technology, and defense sectors of the economy. From laser eye surgery, to cell phone technology, to the illicit import of luxury goods through its private jetties, the IRGC appears to have left virtually no aspect of the Iranian market untapped. Together with its affiliates, the IRGC has secured an estimated U.S. $5 billion in no-bid contracts from the government. This intrusion into the financial sector, particularly in construction, is not new—it began once the Iran-Iraq war ended, when the Guards began playing a significant role in countrywide reconstruction activities. This post-war effort was what helped the IRGC solidify its nationalist credentials, but its subsequent financial ventures were more deeply rooted in self-interest. Specifically, the allocation of a sizable share of the defense budget to the regular forces (Artesh) meant that the IRGC had to become more self-sufficient economically.

It is currently unclear whether this growing economic primacy has produced a backlash among more-traditional commercial sectors. The IRGC may have been able to skillfully co-opt existing companies into its orbit through subcontracts, thereby mitigating dissent and preserving its aura as a nationalist, rather than purely commercial, entity. In many respects, this model replicates the preexisting structures of the religious bonyads, allowing the IRGC's business ventures to be seen as "militarized bonyads" and part of a broader effort to displace the clerical elite from the Republic's economic and political space.

Endowed with this economic and political might, the IRGC is perhaps the sole institution in Iran that can both enforce and breach any "red lines." The most notable example of this dynamic at work is the IRGC's abrupt closure of Imam Khomenei Airport on its opening day, May 9, 2004. The IRGC claimed that the TAV, the Turkish-led consortium selected to operate the airport, presented a security risk to the state by placing foreign workers at a sensitive transportation node. On May 11, the IRGC ordered the TAV to remove its personnel and equipment from Iran. This episode caused significant international embarrassment for Iran, damaged its bilateral relations with Turkey, and hastened the growing impotence of the Khatami administration by forcing the impeachment of his transportation minister. Some observers suspected that the IRGC's action had an economic motive: When the TAV won the tender to operate the airport, the losing bidder reportedly was an Iranian firm with close IRGC ties. In addition, the IRGC may have sought total oversight of the airport's operations because the airport was serving as a key transportation hub in its illicit smuggling activities.

This strong-arm preference for no-bid tenders, monopolization of key industrial sectors, and control of an illicit shadow economy has not gone uncontested within the IRGC and by entities outside the IRGC. Indeed, it raises the larger problem of treating the IRGC as a coherent body, one whose members act in unison across a range of issues. In practice, this is hardly the case. Certainly, there is a large body of opinion within the IRGC that resists greater financial transparency in Iran's economy and Iran's integration into the World Trade Organization (WTO), arguing that these changes would erode the isolation that has thus far empowered the IRGC. At the same time, there are voices that challenge the dominant IRGC narrative of a return to the "golden age" (marked, for example, by the confrontational stridency and insularity of the 1980s). Alarmed by the increasing flight of Iranian capital to Dubai, these voices argue that the IRGC needs to harness, rather than resist, globalization and should extend its arm into international business partnerships.

On the political front, there is also a pragmatic IRGC current. This one emanates from retired Brigadier General Mohammad Baqer Qalibaf, whose near-flawless credentials include war service in the IRGC Air Force; a stint as commander of the Law Enforcement Forces (LEF), where he garnered acclaim for curtailing the excesses of the vigilante "pressure groups" (such as Ansar-e Hezbollah); and, more recently, serving as the mayor of Tehran. Qalibaf fared well in the 2005 presidential elections and has argued that Iran needs a "Muslim Reza Khan"—a Muslim version of the first Shah of Iran, who overthrew the Qajar dynasty and implemented a series of broad-ranging socioeconomic reforms. Aside from his relative political moderation, Qalibaf is an advocate of the IRGC's integration into the global economic order; he reportedly traveled to Zurich at the invitation of a Swiss cement company to explore a business partnership. While Qalibaf is the front-runner of this network, less-known IRGC figures along the network's fringes may be preparing to challenge the hard-liners' domination in the 2009 presidential elections. Many of these, disenchanted with Larijani's tenure as Iran's nuclear point man and the economic isolation of Iran, may be more predisposed to negotiate with the West.

The Iranian Economy: Oil Dependency, Key Actors, and Policies

In trying to fathom the interplay among interest groups, politics, national security, religion, economic policy, and social policy, the general precept "to follow the money" may be especially relevant in Iran compared with other states. In the factionalized Iranian system, the distribution and availability of the country's oil revenues may have a pronounced effect on the regime's speed in making decisions and the degree to which it is compelled to rely on public acquiescence in making decisions: In periods of greater financial liquidity, the regime can "buy off" potential dissent on unpopular policies. In addition, an understanding of these dynamics is important for informing future sanctions policies and assessing their impact.[5]

Two aspects of these dynamics are of particular importance: the peculiar dilemmas and paradoxes associated with Iran's oil-dependent economy, and how successfully Iran's governmental economic organs have grappled with these issues—particularly the degree to which their policies have empowered particular segments of the elite.

Oil Export Dependency and Its Pathologies

That the Iranian economy is heavily driven by oil—its production, value, and exports—is, of course, well known. On average, each increase of 1 percent in Iran's oil export value increases GDP growth by nearly one-quarter of 1 percent; and Iran's recent, relatively high annual growth rate of 5 to 6 percent has been largely driven by increased oil export revenues. Iran's oil export earnings are high, totaling roughly $60 billion in 2007 and constituting 35 percent of GDP. Many aspects of the relationship between oil and Iran's macroeconomy are classic examples of the symptoms displayed by the so-called "resource curse," or "Dutch disease," economic pathology:

1. development of a scarce resource that commands large economic rents for the endowed economy and from the rest of the world
2. a resulting surfeit of internal liquidity and capital inflows that boosts the exchange rate, attracts capital and labor to the resource-favored sector, and inflates domestic demand
3. in turn, price inflation and the siphoning away of productive factors from the non-favored sectors, leading to impeded development of a more balanced, stable, multisector economy.

Aside from these aspects, the Iranian case has some unique aspects. For example, there is the perversely circular relationship between oil exports, GDP, and domestic consumption: Oil exports increase GDP; increased GDP increases domestic consumption of oil, gasoline,

---

[5]   For a recent inquiry into the effectiveness of sanctions on Iran, see United States Government Accounting Office, 2007.

and other refined products; and increased domestic consumption of these products tends to decrease oil exports because total production of crude oil is flat. This sequence is aggravated by a long-standing, politically sensitive policy of heavily subsidizing domestic energy consumption. Thus, the elasticity of energy consumption with respect to changes in income tends to be higher than it would be if full (opportunity) cost pricing of energy prevailed. A further perverse consequence is that because Iran's domestic refining capacity is limited, increases in domestic consumption of refined products generate increased imports rather than increased domestic production and employment. Finally, the reason why domestic production of crude oil is flat is that Iran is reluctant to allow—let alone encourage—the foreign investment and foreign technology needed to exploit proven reserves more fully and to explore more actively to enlarge the pool of reserves.

Iran's oil exports are relatively insensitive to changes in world oil prices. Indeed, the effect of oil prices on Iran's oil exports is slightly negative. While suggestive, this result is not statistically significant: An increase of $1 per barrel in the price of oil leads to a decrease of 11,000 barrels per day (or 0.5 percent) in the volume of Iranian oil exports— an important paradox in the Iranian version of Dutch disease.

In 2006, Iran's oil exports, which were about 2.5 million barrels per day (from production of about 4.0 million barrels per day), generated foreign exchange earnings of $50 billion; and its earnings in 2007 are projected to be over $60 billion. Yet the diversity and complexity of the Iranian system make the flow of these earnings difficult to track. Figures 2.2, 2.3, and 2.4 depict revenue flows and disbursement among ministries drawn from information on the public Website of Iran's Management and Planning Organization.[6] Table 2.1 shows the

---

[6]   See Management and Planning Organization of Iran, 2007. Governmental resources include the government's general income obtained from taxes, and yields from capital assets that include (among other things) part of oil revenues and yields from financial assets. "Other" is a consolidation of governmental entities for which the total incomes and expenditures constitute less than 2 percent of total governmental resources. These governmental entities include (among others) Assembly of Experts, Expediency Council, Ministry of Cooperative, Guardian Council, Ministry of Justice, Department of Environment, Parliament, Management and Planning Organization, Cultural Heritage Organization, Ministry of Labor and Social Affairs, Ministry of Foreign Affairs, Ministry of Industries and Mines,

Figure 2.2
Flow of Funds: Iranian National Budget, 2007

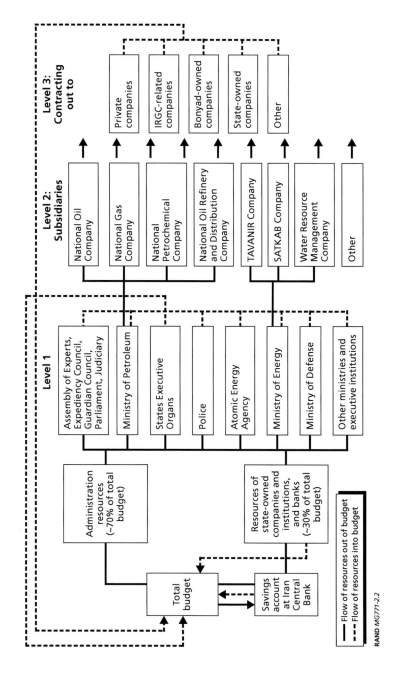

RAND MG771-2.2

Figure 2.3
Flow of Funds: Projected Government Revenue, 2007

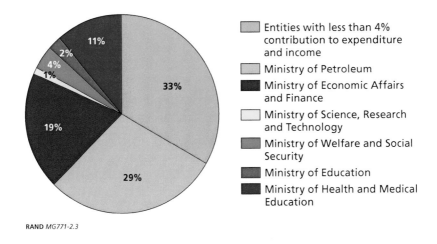

RAND *MG771-2.3*

Figure 2.4
Flow of Funds: Projected Government Spending, 2007

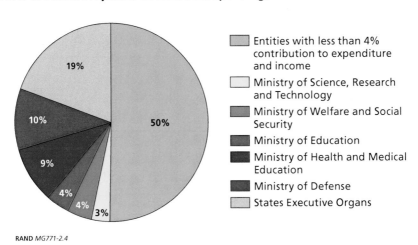

RAND *MG771-2.4*

Ministry of Commerce, Physical Education Organization, Atomic Energy Agency, Ministry of Housing and Urban Development, Office of the President, Foundation of Martyrs and Veteran Affairs, Ministry of Intelligence and Security, Ministry of Islamic Culture and Guidance, Radio and Television, Ministry of Interior, and Judiciary.

Table 2.1
Budgetary Funds: Ministry Sources and Recipients

Name	Total Revenue (rials)		Total Expenditure (rials)	
	Amount	Percent	Amount	Percent
Ministry of Petroleum	203,114,569	29	982,379	0
Ministry of Economic Affairs and Finance	13,024,047	19	1,976,503	0
Ministry of Agriculture and Rural Development	7,068,807	1	11,122,400	2
Police	2,977,800	0	13,535,660	2
Ministry of Education and Training	573,495	0	13,783,746	2
Ministry of Roads and Transport	218,776	0	16,998,700	2
Ministry of Science, Research and Technology	6,445,824	1	19,029,461	3
Ministry of Welfare and Social Security	1,701,000	0	26,599,314	4
Ministry of Education	960,454	0	27,740,254	4
Ministry of Health and Medical Education	30,462,665	4	64,888,364	9
Ministry of Defense	11,230,950	2	69,035,426	10
States Executive Organs	76,977,361	11	134,829,934	19
Other	197,951,357	33	236,741,475	44
Total	691,827,731	100	691,827,733	100

SOURCE: Based on numbers from Management and Planning Organization of Iran, 2007.

ministry sources for and recipients of budgetary funds. It should be noted, however, that these data are only partially helpful in that they show the ministries' *total* income, and there is no way to discern the portion from oil revenues. Moreover, we have no way to capture the expansive shadow economy, much of which appears to be increasingly controlled by IRGC or IRGC-affiliated entities. What our graphics are able to do, however, is suggest the profound complexity of a bureaucratic system beset by multiple conflicts of interest—certainly among the recipients of oil largesse, but also among institutions charged with formulating and implementing economic policy.

Economic Policies and Institutions: Complexity and Redundancy

While the government's desire for control over the economy remains relatively high, two sets of policy frameworks currently govern Iran's economic policy: (1) the 20-year long-term perspective drawn by the Supreme Leadership and (2) the five-year development plans (FYDPs) prepared and implemented by the government in power. The long-term perspective is a virtual guideline associated with macroeconomic targets set for the long run; the successive FYDPs are designed in conformity with the long-term perspective, their goal being to adjust and rectify structural problems within the country that have become hindrances to Iran's economic development and a healthy economic policy. Ever since the 1990 introduction of the first FYDP, which had an objective of promoting reconstruction, development, and liberalization of the economy, two successive governments, those of Rafsanjani and Khatami, have stated their intentions to tackle inflation, unemployment, inefficiency, and incompetency through structural reform of the country's war-ravaged economy. In both administrations, however, the results were severely lacking; in fact, most of these problems worsened.

Both administrations also recognized that Iran badly needed to reduce its dependency on oil export revenues, curtail government overspending, and adjust monetary policy to control inflation. Following an absence of more than one decade, foreign direct investment (FDI) was sought seriously by the government—exhibited by fierce debates in the Majles—as a booster to invigorate the economy. The Law on Attraction and Promotion of Foreign Investment (LAPFI), a fossil legislation introduced in 1955, was the only tool provided to entice foreign investors, who, it turned out, sought what they thought to be better and more-promising opportunities in places such as Dubai. This

comparative disadvantage pushed the Khatami government to prepare and introduce the Foreign Investment Promotion and Protection
Act (FIPPA) in 2000. A relaxation of trade policies and a subsequent
attempt to unify multiple foreign exchange rates then occurred as further key elements of economic reform. The exchange rate was finally
unified during Khatami's second presidency as an instrument for promoting a more liberalized economy.

Today, it is no exaggeration to state that roughly one dozen governmental bodies are mobilized in the process of economic policy decisionmaking. This situation presents the regime, whatever its political
disposition, with serious challenges in any attempt to coordinate the
state's economic policies. The primary authorities involved in this decisionmaking process are

- the ministers with responsible portfolios
- the Majles as a whole and its relevant commissions individually
- the Supreme Economic Council chaired by the president
- the Guardian Council with vetting powers to reject legislation by
  the Majles and the Expediency Council as an advisory board to
  the Supreme Leader

On the issue of attracting foreign investment, several entities play
a role:

- High Council for Investment, chaired by the minister of Econ-
  omy and Finance
- High Council of Free Trade Zones, working directly beneath the
  president (specifically, for free trade zones, or FTZs)
- Supervisory Board for the Attraction and Protection of Foreign
  Investment
- Organization for Investment, Economic and Technical Assistance
  of Iran (OIETAI), a subsidiary of the Ministry of Economy and
  Finance

Other relevant institutions are the ministries of the Interior, Labor, and Social Affairs; the Customs Agency; the Iranian Privatization Organization (POI); and the Central Bank of Iran (CBI) (Bank-e Markazi).

The semi-official or even non-official bodies—such as the local Basij units and the Chamber of Commerce, Industry and Mines, which partially represent the private sector—get involved as pressure groups to exert influence on key decisionmaking bodies. In between stand the official bonyads (such as the Bonyad-e Mostazafan) and the recently attention-getting IRGC subsidiaries that have high stakes in the semi-state economy but also enjoy strong personal relationships with key political players.

Disarray and Dysfunction in Economic Policy Execution

Implementation of certain policies has been hampered by the complexity arising from the overlapping and competing governmental and semi-governmental entities and agencies that have existed since the early days of the Islamic Revolution. At times, a government has made decisions that contradicted each other and, in the end, undermined the designed effect on the economy. The actual use of the Oil Stabilization Fund (OSF), created under the fourth FYDP, displays clear signs of inconsistency with the original, sensible objective. The OSF has been a constant source of political debate and power struggles among various factions, usually leading to sponsorship of additional government spending. Lack of coordination within the government, associated with the government's rather common flip-flops on interpretation and implementation of OSF policy, has not impressed foreign capitals. FDI thus has not materialized in the way it was supposed to.

Nor has Iran's privatization target been met. According to an International Monetary Fund (IMF) report of March 2007, complicated regulatory and legal structures and weak political support have prevented effective implementation of the previously ongoing privatization program since the late 1980s. While ostensibly still promoting privatization, the government has continued to provide favors and preferential treatment to state-owned entities—a practice likely to dissuade the capital market from participating in initial public offerings (IPOs). Moreover, companies owned by or affiliated with the IRGC, or subcontracted by it, have been increasing their role in the economy. Conflict between the stipulation of the Constitution's Article 44 and the government policy had virtually put the program in hibernation for years until recently, when the Supreme Leader issued a comprehensive directive to resolve the matter. The privatization program is now expected to get back on track while firmly excluding from privatization the upstream oil sector, crucial infrastructure, and some of the state-owned banks.

Discrepancies between the government and the Majles on the same issue have abridged certain policies, as is evident in the normalization of the fuel and utility prices. Toward the final year of Khatami's presidency, the Majles suspended the privatization program. The additional cost for importing oil products, inter alia gasoline, then had to be allocated, depending solely on the OSF as the resource, for more than three years, until a rationing system was introduced in summer 2007. Suggested reform of the buyback agreement scheme also fell into this trap.

Currently, under the Ahmadinejad presidency, the focus of Iran's priorities has shifted from structural reform to reducing social and regional disparities. Distortion of the economy, consisting of extensive administrative controls on prices and interest rates and aggravated by heavy government spending (especially by Ahmadinejad), is worsening every year through the provision of subsidies, both obvious and hidden, on various goods and services. Ahmadinejad's strong commitment to drawing down bank interest rates in order to tame inflation to single digits—which has jeopardized the independence and function of the CBI—is another policy that is likely to eventually prove self-defeating. Inflation, fueled by burgeoning revenues from oil exports, has been galvanized rather than tamed.

In the Islamic Republic, therefore, excessive political control—or perhaps, put more accurately, political interference—in both policy decisionmaking and policy implementation is spoiling the economy. For the elite, the economy remains a "tool" for gaining greater power—an important feature of the larger processes of decisionmaking and factional maneuvering among the leaders.

The Elite's Political Culture: Factionalism and Informality

Beneath the office of the Supreme Leader and transcending the complicated structure of the defense establishment and the representative institutions (such as the Majles), there is a highly pluralistic political system comprising more than 200 parties and countless informal networks. As an arena for intense factional maneuvering, this landscape is very much a by-product of Ayatollah Khomeini's approach to governing Iran as a Shiite Islamic republic. This approach grew out of the need to reconcile two frequently contradictory currents underpinning Khomeini's political philosophy of the Islamic republic: an isolationist, combative, and excessively dogmatic current, which might be termed *Jihadi,* and a more integrative, flexible, and pluralistic current, best described as *Ijtihadi* in reference to the Islamic juridical process of applying "independent reasoning" to the sacred religious texts.

Since the mid-1980s, the interplay of these currents has produced three convoluted and overlapping factional coalitions, which we can roughly label *conservative, reformist,* and *pragmatist.* All three of these have operated within the Islamic ideological and political framework laid down by Khomeini, and their members have come from similar religious and social backgrounds, cutting across the traditional socioeconomic layers and class barriers that prevailed in Iranian politics and society prior to the Islamic Revolution. However, once the Islamic order was consolidated, the question for Khomeini was how to secure its long-term viability. He seems to have intended from the beginning to promote an Ijtihadi dimension along with his Jihadi efforts to allow for the degree of domestic political pluralism and foreign policy flexibility needed to help reconstruct Iran as an internationally acceptable, strong, and modern Islamic state. It was in this context that his revolutionary/Jihadi supporters underwent a major metamorphosis shortly after the triumph of the revolution, giving rise to three informal clusters:

- *The conservative/Jihadi cluster.* This first cluster, also called the revolutionary cluster, coalesced around such figures as Ali Khamenei and Mohammad Reza Mahdavi Kani. This entity argued for a patriarchal Islamic government, consolidation of the revolution's gains, preservation of a traditional style of life, promotion of self-sufficiency with no dependence on the outside world, and cultural purity. Among its constituents, it counts the rural population, the IRGC (although not in its entirety, as discussed above), and certain radical clerical figures.

- *The reformist/Ijtihadi cluster.* This second cluster began to form in 1987 around such leaders as Mehdi Karrubi and Mohammad Khatami. This entity united in its support for a pluralist, democratic Islamic political system. Some of its leading figures, most importantly Khatami, argued for promotion of civil society, relaxation of political and social control, economic openness, cultural renaissance, and more interaction with the outside world. Members of this cluster were inspired by such Iranian thinkers as Ali Shariati and, later, Abdul Karim Soroush, who synthesized Islamic moral concepts with modern Enlightenment political philosophy to argue that there was no inherent tension between democracy and Islamic society. But some leaders who tended to be more realists than idealists emphasized the importance of maintaining a balance of power in domestic politics.[7]
- *The centrist/pragmatist cluster.* The third cluster, which crystallized around Rafsanjani, generally stood between the first and second clusters and organized itself within two parties—the Executives of Construction Party (Hezbe Kargozaran Sazandegi), which supported the reformist approach to culture, and the Justice and

---

[7]   The reformist camp is very divided today. The most liberal reformists are in the Participation Front Party (Jebhe-ye Mosharekat), which is led institutionally by Mohammad Khatami, brother of former President Khatami, and intellectually by Saeed Hajjarian and his associates. The second group, which is the most influential and disciplined party, is the Organization of Strivers of the Islamic Revolution (Sazmane Mojahedine Enghelab Eslami). The third group, which is non-clerical, is the Solidarity Party (Hezbe Hambastegi). Its major figure is Ibrahim Asgharzadeh, who was one of the leaders in the 1979 hostage-taking fiasco, although he now asserts that such action is detrimental to world peace and Iran's foreign relations. Indeed, many leading reformists are now critical of the radical conservatism they displayed in the first few years of the revolution. The least modern group amongst the reformists remains the Assembly of Assertive Clerics (AAC), which is led by Mohammad Mousavi Khoeiniha and is mainly affiliated with Ayatollah Hossein Ali Montazeri.

Development Party (Hezbe E'tedal va Tose'eh), which leaned toward the conservatives on cultural issues. The camp as a whole was inspired by the intellectual work of a number of economic academics and believed in economic modernization from above (the so-called China model). It argued for increased technical and financial cooperation with the West, including the United States, but had little evident interest in democratizing politics. It has flip-flopped on many issues, leading to accusations of opportunism from its rivals among the conservative/Jihadi cluster, who depict themselves quite literally and self-righteously as "principlists" that have remained steadfast to the revolution's ideals. The pragmatists have traditionally derived support from the merchant class (bazaari), students, urban middle classes, and technocrats.

Since the death of Khomeini, each current has had its heyday, enjoying its own period of formal political power:

- 1989–1997: Rafsanjani and the centrist/pragmatist cluster, who presided over Iran's post-war reconstruction
- 1997–2005: Khatami and the reformist/Ijtihadi cluster, who emphasized the growth of civil society and the so-called "dialogue of civilizations"
- 2005–present: Ahmadinejad and the conservative/Jihadi current and the IRGC.

It is important to note that all three factional clusters have grown to act within the Jihadi-Ijtihadi framework promoted by Khomeini as part of what has been deeply embedded in the Shiite theological approach to earthly existence. They have, on the one hand, engaged in power struggles and, on the other hand, accommodated and overlapped with one another. The conservatives have upheld the ideological purity of Khomeini's legacy while proving to be quite pragmatic and reformist when needed. The reformists have sought to popularize and pluralize the legacy and make it palatable to the international community without losing sight of their organic links with the conservatives. And the pragmatists have straddled the two whenever it was opportune to do so. There has been almost a routine fluidity of movement among the clusters, with some members changing cluster allegiance quite frequently, and leaders remaining in consultation meetings with one another from time to time to adopt a coordinated position to face a serious threat. As such, they have all operated within the limits needed to preserve the Islamic regime.

Another defining feature of what can be termed *inter-cluster operability* is that the dominant conservative current has embraced as its own a number of policy formulations and practices of the pragmatists and reformists. Conservatives have done this because they know they must change with the requirements of a changing Iran and world or risk the future of the Islamic regime. In a sense, the need for the politics of regime preservation has led them to acquiesce to some pluralist changes, with the result that Iran can no longer be regarded as strictly a theocratic state. Whatever President Ahmadinejad's Jihadi rhetoric, he ultimately has little choice but to carry many of his Ijtihadi opponents with him, much as Khomeini did 20 years earlier.

Currently, the principal axis of contention lies between the conservative/Jihadi camp and the pragmatists (the reform camp is, to a large degree, a politically exhausted force, having grown disenchanted and demoralized in the second half of the Khatami era). One could argue that the struggle between the pragmatists and conservatives has always been at the forefront of Iran's political struggles and that the Khatami era was simply a "respite" for the conservatives—a time to regroup and reorganize for success against the Rafsanjani camp. Iran's "third revolution" is therefore an intensely factional affair and, perhaps most important of all, one in which the conservatives are wielding nuclear power as a domestic weapon to subvert and outmaneuver their rivals.

Factional Dynamics at Work: The Nuclear Case Study

Among its proponents, Iran's nuclear program, particularly the retention of an indigenous fuel cycle, has attained a symbolic resonance comparable to that of then–Prime Minister Mohammad Mossadegh's nationalization of Iranian oil production in 1951. In both cases, energy resources encapsulate the large themes of modernity, sovereignty, self-sufficiency, and non-submission to Western control. In this respect, Ahmadinejad's populist embrace of nuclear energy as Iran's "indisputable right" follows the Mossadegh model—like the deposed prime minister, Ahmadinejad is using domestic energy as leverage over his domestic rivals, aiming to consolidate his position at home and to build support among his power base, particularly in the rural periphery. The nuclear program thus provides an important case study for observing how public opinion, consensus, informal networks, and external pressure shape regime behavior.

It is important to note first that the regime's deliberations over the nuclear program from 1982 to 2002 were largely immune to considerations of public support because the research was conducted in utter secrecy. Even within the regime's technocratic core, there were complaints up until 2003 that real experts were being excluded from any rational discussion of the program's risks and benefits. Similarly, Iran's nuclear drive appears to have been insensitive to both pressures and incentives from the United States. In 1999, at the very moment that U.S.-Iran relations were warming and then–Secretary of State Madeleine Albright delivered her apology for the 1953 CIA-sponsored coup against Mossadegh, Tehran was receiving critical technical expertise from Pakistani nuclear mastermind A. Q. Khan. Thus, it was not so much the direct threat of U.S. regime change that impelled Tehran to pursue enrichment and a possible weapons capability, but more likely the desire for a "hedge" against unforeseen threats and a deterrent against their more proximate foe, Iraq, as well as the need for energy diversification.

With the 2003 public disclosure of the nuclear program by the Mujahidin-e Khalq (MeK) organization, the program's motives, scope, and opportunity costs became subject to greater transparency and scrutiny. Public opinion was initially a *background* factor in nuclear decisionmaking, not necessarily a *driver* or *constraint*. For the regime, public dissatisfaction with the costs of the program or sanctions associated with it could not be ignored. Public opinion was thus invoked as an important consideration by both factions[8]—by hard-liners, as a reason for pursuing the program regardless of pressure, and by pragmatists, as a factor for caution. Yet in manipulating the issue, the regime has, ironically, become a captive of public opinion. Depending on their respective inclinations, the conservatives, who are appealing to a largely fundamentalist constituency, see a retreat from their position as being constrained by public opinion; whereas the pragmatists, who are appealing to a more middle-class constituency, see pursuit of the current course as risking a high-speed economic collision, with consequent damage to the regime.

Despite its solicitation of public opinion, the regime has neither permitted nor encouraged real debate about the energy rationale of the nuclear program in the context of alternative policies and options. Instead, it has made repeated and misleading references to "national consensus" when it really means "elite consensus." While most Iranians agree on Iran's unrestricted right to seek modern technologies, consensus clearly fades when the topic turns to what Iranians are willing to pay for the program's continuation in terms of sanctions, loss of investment confidence, capital flight, and estrangement from the international community.[9] Nonetheless, Iranian negotiators have argued that their hands are tied on the nuclear issue by the unanimity of support within the public and the Majles. The negotiators invoke this pressure to pressure their European negotiating partners. The result is the kind of brinksmanship, a "managed crisis" just short of conflict, that characterized the negotiations from 2003 to 2005.

In addition to the broader public, there are other important constituencies and "audiences" in the nuclear arena. The strongest supporters of Iran's nuclear drive are those that stand to lose the most from its

---

[8]   For more on factional views of the nuclear issue, see Chubin, 2007. Also see Chubin, 2006.

[9]   See especially Chubin and Litwak, 2003; and Michael Herzog, 2006. See also Abdin, 2006. A 2006 poll (Zogby and Reader's Digest, 2006) reports that 41 percent of Iranians put reforming the economy before having a nuclear capability (27 percent). The poll also reveals a country divided on many issues. See also Khalaj, 2006. A 2007 poll (World Public Opinion, 2007) reports that 84 percent of Iranians think it is very important for Iran to have a full fuel cycle and 89 percent think it is very important for Iran to have a nuclear energy program.

termination. Foremost among these is Iran's Atomic Energy Organization (AEO), which oversees the program's scientific and technical dimensions. For the AEO, the stakes are especially high; its opposition to any freeze of enrichment stems partly from the detrimental effect such a freeze would have on the retention and employment of scientific personnel. One expert has argued that the costs of suspension for the AEO could exceed U.S. $5 billion and 15 years of effort. The argument from a technical standpoint is that elimination of one of the five phases of nuclear production "will render all other phases and the efforts of scientists in past years ineffective." Additionally, the AEO argues for an unconstrained program on security grounds: "If we do not produce nuclear fuel inside our country, they will use fuel as leverage to threaten our independence and territorial integrity in the future." Unsurprisingly, the head of the AEO is among the most vocal proponents of the program, comparing the quest for indigenous enrichment with the need for food self-sufficiency. His clout within the debate is further strengthened by the fact that the AEO, unlike other bureaucratic organs, such as the Majles, is not subject to political turnover and thus can maintain a consistent line and constant presence.

The other principal constituency for the nuclear drive is the IRGC, which provides security for all nuclear-related installations and, given its current role as custodian of Iran's ballistic missile arsenal, would likely exert command and control over any nuclear weapons. Since we do not have access to a debate about nuclear *weapons* within the leadership itself, we can only conjecture the role of the Guards in such a debate. Senior IRGC officials have expressed scepticism about arms control agreements but have not publicly stated an institutional view about nuclear weapons as such. Like most of the hard-liners in the regime, they have supported the nuclear program; but they appear to be especially predisposed to its continuation: The IRGC has been the foremost proponent of Iran's "asymmetric warfare" doctrine, which seeks to leverage unconventional tactics and technologies to confront a conventionally superior opponent. During the last phase of the war with Iraq, Guards Commander Mohsen Rezai argued that without nuclear weapons, Iran could not continue the war with any hope of winning.[10] With missiles (which are under IRGC control), an Iranian nuclear option could deter attacks on the homeland and project Iranian power regionally. And it certainly could enhance the IRGC's prestige and primacy over the regular armed forces (Artesh).[11]

The nuclear issue is also used for a purpose that overlaps bureaucratic interests. The pragmatist and conservative clusters have used it as part of a larger negotiation over internal power, patronage, and the country's engagement with the world. The basic positions can be summarized (albeit imperfectly) as follows:

The pragmatists, embodied in the figures of Rafsanjani and former Khatami-era nuclear negotiator Rowhani, see a nuclear capability as a bargaining chip with the United States, their ultimate goal being deeper negotiation of Iran's economic integration with the world—for example, Iran becoming more of a "normal" state in return for abandoning its nuclear ambitions.

The conservative/*Ijtihadi* current, represented by the Supreme Leader, Ahmadinejad, Larijani, and Jalili (the new secretary of the SNCS), perceive the nuclear issue more as an equalizer with the United States, needed to safeguard the fundamentals of the revolution and to ultimately preserve Iran's sovereignty—even if that means enduring international opprobrium and isolation. Aside from its role in this debate about Iran's external standing, the nuclear issue is a factional weapon wielded by the conservative current, especially those in the IRGC. The nationalist discourse on nuclear energy and its attendant economic benefits for the rural poor has enormous value for the IRGC leadership, which has presented itself as a populist, technocratic alternative to the elitism and corruption of the "oil-oligarchy" clustered around Rafsanjani.

It is important to note that these domestic tensions have played out in Iran's inconsistent and erratic negotiating behavior on the nuclear file. Most significantly, the Khatami-era negotiating team,

---

[10]   For a useful and accessible summary of this episode, see Bozorghmehr, 2006. See also Nafisi, 2006, in which Nafisi notes that the incident "reveals the diversity of views on the nuclear issue."

[11]   Gheissari and Nasr, "The Conservative Consolidation," pp. 177, 179, 188.

which included ex-foreign minister Kamal Kharrazi, SCNS Secretary Rowhani, and Rowhani's deputy, Hossein Musavian, has been subjected to extensive pressure since the rise of the conservatives. The most visible manifestation of this crackdown was the arrest of Musavian on espionage charges; his detention was widely interpreted as a response to having crossed a "red line" when he publicly stated to a *Financial Times* reporter that Iran's nuclear negotiations had reached a "dead end." The timing of this leak and the resulting wrath of the IRGC/conservatives was not coincidental—this was precisely the moment in 2005 when Ahmadinejad's supporters had suffered a crushing defeat in the municipal council elections. Musavian's arrest was thus an attempt by the conservatives to reassert themselves domestically, using the nuclear portfolio as their vehicle. To counter this power play, Rowhani and Rafsanjani paid Musavian's bail, and Rafsanjani has recently made a point of being seen in public with him.[12]

In tandem with these domestic dimensions, the nuclear issue has been an integral part of the popular adulation of Iran among public audiences in the Arab world. This dynamic raises the larger issue of how Iran's attempt to curry favor with Arab audiences affects its foreign policy behavior.

Iran's Approach to Its Arab Neighbors: Implications for Iranian Behavior and U.S. Policy

Iran has long pursued a policy of speaking over the heads of Arab regimes, taking its message directly to Arab populations and presenting itself as "more Arab than the Arabs"—traditionally on Palestine, but increasingly also on Iraq. An understanding of the dynamics of Arab perceptions of Iran—both official and public—is critical to U.S. policymaking on the Islamic Republic. Given that U.S. policymakers have been increasingly turning to Arab regimes as interlocutors, interpreters, and allies with respect to Iran, it is crucial that they understand the complex set of local interests and agendas that inform these roles.

---

[12] *BBC Monitoring*, 2007b.

Moreover, the United States cannot separate the challenge of Iran from the Arab sphere, particularly the Arabian Gulf. Iran both influences and is influenced by the perceptions of its Arab neighbors. Specifically, the Iranian government's belief, whether warranted or not, that it can draw support from Arab publics has impelled it toward brinksmanship and bravado in its foreign policy.

Iran's Outreach to Arab Publics

Iran's hyper-activism on pan-Arab issues can be viewed not as proof of Iran's influence in the "Arab street," but, rather, just the opposite: an effort to overcompensate for its fundamental isolation from the rest of the region. Despite Iran's claims to universalism, it remains the odd man out. By its own admission, its attempts to refashion the Arab world in its image have largely failed, as is most clearly illustrated by the fact that its principal Arab Shiite "clients" in the Gulf—formerly, the Islamic Front for the Liberation of Bahrain, the Organization for the Islamic Revolution on the Arabian Peninsula, and the Supreme Council for the Islamic Revolution in Iraq—have all distanced themselves from their erstwhile patron through name changes and/or the more substantial move of goal reorientation.[13]

Under President Ahmadinejad, Iran's outreach to the Arab street has grown especially vociferous and brazen. He has received widespread applause from Arab publics for his populist, grassroots appeal and for being outspokenly critical of the status quo—characteristics that put him in sharp contrast with many of the Arab world's cautious and frequently septuagenarian rulers. For example, at the 2005 Organization of the Islamic Conference (OIC) summit in Mecca, Ahmadinejad made a speech denying the Holocaust in the presence of Saudi Arabia's King Abdullah bin Abdulaziz. To the members of the ruling family of the Kingdom of Saudi Arabia (the al-Saud), who have portrayed themselves as the region's preeminent patrons of the Palestinians, Ahmadinejad's remarks were a brazen act of one-upsmanship.

---

[13] These organizations are now, respectively, the Islamic Action Society, the Saudi-based Reform Movement, and the Supreme Islamic Iraqi Council.

Inside Iran, this "Arabist" posturing has stirred debate. Some of this is based on the arguments of certain IRGC figures that the posturing risks undermining Iran's good trade relations with the Gulf Cooperation Council (GCC). These same figures have criticized recent statements by senior officials warning the GCC states of a massive and indiscriminate retaliation against their civilian infrastructure if the U.S. strikes the Islamic Republic. Recently, debate erupted after an advisor of the Supreme Leader publicly claimed that Bahrain was rightfully a province of Iran.

An important point to be made here is that any appeal garnered by Iran among Arab publics is fragile and subject to rapid fluctuation. Iran's sole attraction among these audiences is likely its belligerent stance on Israel and its implicit criticism of often unpopular Arab regimes, and this attraction can be quickly overshadowed by regional events that are either beyond Iran's control or the result of Iran's strategic incompetence. A notable example is the rapidity with which the collateral acclaim Iran had received in connection with Hizballah's 2006 war with Israel dissipated once Iraq's Saddam Husayn was executed in December 2006, an event the Arab world widely viewed as an attempt engineered by Iran and the United States to diminish Arab identity. A commentator on Iran's Arabic satellite TV appeared perplexed by this reaction from the Arab world; he questioned why the "Arab media are intentionally using the execution of Saddam Husayn to foment sectarian conflict" and concluded that "those who are mourning Saddam ... are worried about their shaky thrones."[14] By 2007, available polling and media surveys had revealed a noticeable drop in Arab public support for Iran—stemming principally from worsening sectarian violence in Iraq. Zogby's 2007 polling of 3,400 Arab respondents in Egypt, Saudi Arabia, Jordan, the United Arab Emirates (UAE), and Lebanon showed that a majority believed Iran's role in Iraq was unhelpful.

To combat anti-Iranian themes in the official Arab media, Iran employs a well-developed architecture of transnational outlets to reach Arab audiences. Although this strategy is now bolstered by recent technological advances, it is not new—the importance of "psychological

---

[14] Open Source Center, 2007.

warfare" has long been a fixation of Iran's revolutionary leadership. For example, in a 2006 Arabic monograph on the subject, *The Role of Media in Political and Cultural Conflict* (Dur Wasa'il al-A'lam fi al-Sira' al-Siyasi wa al-Thaqafi), the Supreme Leader praised the historic role of radio, TV, and other media in cultivating Islamic ideals after the revolution, mobilizing Arab support for Hizballah, and deflecting misrepresentations of the Islamic Republic.

In general, however, Iran's media aspirations in the Arab sphere have fallen short. According to available media surveys, Iran's major transnational Arab media outlet, *Al Alam*, has lagged its pan-Arab competitors, *Al Arabiya* and *Al Jazeera*, in both credibility and popularity.[15] And according to RAND interviews conducted in early 2007, even Iran's Shiite co-religionists in Saudi Arabia's Eastern Province consider the channel heavy handed and too ideological.[16]

Iran and Anti-Shiism

One concern expressed by Arab states, especially in the Gulf, is that Iran is pursuing a divisive sectarian policy, attempting to agitate Arab Shiite populations and inspire them to greater activism and even militancy. Such fears are not new; they date back to the post-revolutionary period. Yet the prospect of a U.S. withdrawal from Iraq, Iran's nuclear ambitions, and recent Iranian statements about filling the regional "power vacuum" have only intensified Arab alarm. A recent editorial in *Al Sharq Al Awsat* lambasted Iran for behaving like a "sect" and for embracing the same "colonialist logic of vacuum-filling" that informed

---

[15] According to a poll conducted by Iran's own state broadcasting research arm of 1,400 adults in Beirut and southern Lebanon following the Israel-Hizballah conflict, only 22 percent of respondents stated that they watched *Al Alam*. In 2004, however, an Intermedia Survey reported that 78 percent of Iraqi viewers had access to satellite dishes and that *Al Alam*'s total audience reach was at 15 percent, compared with over 60 percent for the most popular channels, *Al Arabiya* and *Al Jazeera*. Moreover, the station received only single figures for reliability and importance as a source of information. (*BBC Monitoring*, 2008)

[16] RAND discussions with Shiite religious leaders and activists in Qatif, Dammam, and al-Ahsa, Eastern Province, Saudi Arabia, March 15–20, 2007.

the U.S. intervention in the Middle East after Britain's "east of Suez" withdrawal.[17]

Here again, such rumblings are more accurately seen as windows into deeper problems of Arab political illegitimacy and governance. Nowhere is this more apparent than in Bahrain, where the regime has traditionally used the specter of Iranian omnipotence to portray any moves toward reform and democratization as "sectarian" or "Iranian backed." Yet the real challenge posed by Iranian-backed Shiite actors, such as the Lebanese Hizballah, lies not so much in their sectarian threat to Sunnis per se, but in their populist, non-sectarian challenge to the old political order. Analogies drawn by Egyptian oppositionists to "Nasser 1956—Nasrallah 2006" provide a stark example of this dynamic at work.[18] Similarly, recent reports of conversions to Shiism by Arab Sunnis are more a reflection of status quo frustration than the result of any concerted proselytizing efforts by Iran.

For their part, Iranian leaders are generally careful not to make statements that will inflame sectarian tensions—for example, referring to the Taliban and al-Qaeda as takfiris,[19] extremists, or reactionaries, but rarely as Sunnis. Such distinctions are probably made with domestic audiences in mind; when Majles Speaker Haddad-Adel addressed the largely Sunni population of Sistan-va Baluchestan in November 2006, he emphasized the absence of discord in Iran between Sunnis and Shiites by pointing to Iran's support for both Shiite Hizballah and Sunni Hamas.[20]

Nonetheless, some Arab regimes have played up the sectarian character of the Iranian challenge, probably to curry popular support for what is essentially a balance-of-power strategy against Iran. As noted by F. Gregory Gause III, anti-Shiism is a way to "sell" an anti-Iranian policy and dampen public enthusiasm for Iran's defiant nuclear

---

[17] Al-Hasan, 2007.

[18] Valbjørn and Bank, 2007, p. 7.

[19] *Takfiri* is an appellation for Muslims who excommunicate other Muslims as unbelievers. For Jihadi ideologues, violence against persons excommunicated this way is legitimate.

[20] Valbjørn and Bank, 2007, pp. 10–11.

posture.[21] Thus, we see in Saudi Arabia the recirculation of old anti-Shiite fatawa, many of which originated in the Saudi-Iranian ideological "cold war" of the 1980s. One key example is the renewed popularity of an anti-Shiite book written shortly after the revolution by an influential Syrian-born Saudi cleric. This tract was quoted extensively by Abu Musab al-Zarqawi in a four-hour diatribe recorded shortly before his death in June 2006.[22]

The most immediate victims of this trend are Arab Shiite populations, especially on the Arabian Peninsula. Increasingly, Bahraini, Saudi, and to a lesser extent Kuwaiti Shiites have been portrayed by Salafi hard-liners and some regime officials either as disloyal "fifth columns" for Iran or as agents of sectarian discord (fitna).[23] A notable example is Egyptian President Hosni Mubarak's televised declaration that Arab Shiites' "loyalty is always to Iran" and "not to their countries."[24] More recently, a senior Saudi establishment cleric attacked Saudi Arabia's leading Shiite figure, Hassan al-Saffar, for allegedly promoting excommunication (takfir) of Sunnis.[25]

Such accusations, however, are unjustified. Gulf Shiites generally regard Iran with spiritual and emotional affinity, rather than as a political model for emulation, and have pushed for cross-sectarian dialogue. Many appear unwilling to jeopardize hard-won political gains made in the 1990s to serve as Tehran's retaliatory proxies. Shiite intellectuals

---

[21] Gause, 2007.

[22] The book (al-Gharib, 1988) is by Muhammad 'Abdallah al-Gharib, believed by many analysts to be a pseudonym for Muhammad Surur Zayn al-Abidin, an influential Syrian-born cleric who taught in Burayda. Al-Zarqawi, n.d., is the transcript of al-Zarqawi's audio recording.

[23] Wehry, 2007; also Jones, 2007.

[24] Mubarak's statement was carried on *Al Arabiya* TV, on April 9, 2006. Also see Anon., 2006. In Egypt, this tactic is not new; recall that the Islamic Revolution animated Muslim Brotherhood activists, prompting the Sadat regime to emphasize its narrow sectarian motives throughout the state-controlled media (Mathee, 1986).

[25] al-Saffar, 2007.

on the Peninsula have also been vocal critics of vilayet-e faqih, with a resonance that extends well beyond the Gulf.[26]

Despite their protestations of loyalty, however, Gulf Shiites perceive a palpable stall in domestic reform initiatives, which many attribute to Washington's recent focus on building Arab support against Iran rather than promoting democracy.[27] Ironically, this loss of momentum, combined with the hardening of Sunni opinion, could actually reinforce the Shiites' sectarian identity, radicalizing their increasingly youthful populations and creating new openings for Iranian influence that might not otherwise exist.

Understanding these multidimensional effects is of critical importance for U.S. policymakers seeking Arab support against Iran. Every Arab state that elects to align itself with the United States against Iran—whether as a stalwart military ally or a diplomatic interlocutor—has a deep set of domestic and regional calculations in mind that may diverge completely from Washington's calculations. In consequence, U.S. policies toward Iran could reverberate in the Arab sphere in unintended ways and, perhaps, to the potential detriment of other U.S. interests.

Iran's Negotiating Style

The analysis of the previous section highlights the problem of U.S. policymakers viewing Iran through the lenses of other Arab nations. Yet interpersonal negotiations with Iranians are also fraught with pitfalls—as well as opportunities. According to a Persian-speaking Japanese businessman with broad and sustained experience in the Islamic Republic:

---

[26] Examples include Tawfiq al-Sayf's *Nathariyat al-Sulta fi al-Fiqh al-Shi'i* (Theories of Political Power in Shiite Jurisprudence) (al-Sayf, 2002), and Hassan al-Saffar's *Al-Madhhab wa al-Watan* (Sect and Homeland) (al-Saffar, 2006).

[27] In a February 2006 interview with the author, a prominent Salafi reformer and legal expert in Riyadh warned that tensions with Iran would result in a curtailment of social and political reforms; this was subsequently echoed in follow-up interviews with other reformists, activists, and intellectuals in Jeddah, Riyadh, and the Eastern Province in March 2007.

> Negotiating with Iranian business counterparts is said to be stimulating, since they always see room in negotiation, as opposed to the business-like yet dry negotiating style of "take it or leave it" that prevails with some of their Arab neighbors.

This comment raises the larger issues of the "uniqueness" and "normalcy" of negotiating with Iran and, more fundamentally, the necessity of talking to Iranians as a matter of policy.

On the second of these points, the U.S.'s long aversion to talking with Iran has squandered two windows of opportunity to reduce the decades-long animosity between the two states. The first window occurred in 2002, immediately following the Taliban's ascendancy in Afghanistan, when Iran offered diplomatic support on Afghanistan to the United States. At the 2001 Bonn talks on Afghanistan, Iranian diplomacy proved critical in brokering a power-sharing agreement among Afghan factions and tempering the Northern Alliance's insistence on dominance in the new ministries. On the margins of subsequent meetings, Iranian representatives offered to assist the United States in rebuilding the Afghan army and appeared willing to discuss issues beyond Afghanistan, as well. U.S. policymakers gave the Iranians no response on these offers.

Fearing that the United States had its cross-hairs on Tehran after overthrowing Saddam Husayn, Iranian leaders made their second proposal in May 2003. By various accounts, this initiative included Iran's severance of ties with its Levantine terrorist allies, the conversion of the Lebanese Hizballah into a purely sociopolitical party, discussions on the surrender of al-Qaeda operatives in Iran's custody, and entering into serious bilateral negotiations on Iran's nuclear program. Here again, Iran's offer was met with silence.

Gratitude and fear were the twin motives animating these Iranian overtures. Today, both of these motives are absent in Tehran's worldview, replaced by a newfound sense of strategic confidence. Added to this confidence is the plummeting U.S. regional credibility since the fall of Saddam, as well as Iran's perception that the U.S. entanglement in Iraq and, to a lesser extent, Afghanistan constrains the United States both militarily and diplomatically from acting against the Islamic

Republic. Even Tehran's moderate proponents of engagement are faced with the indisputable fact that the Khatami-era attempts at dialogue with the United States yielded little fruit. All of this casts serious doubt on any expectations of a diplomatic breakthrough or grand bargain.

Given such prospects, it may appear that any attempts at negotiation are pointless, particularly given the current regime's ideological predisposition and the seeming absence of any Iranian counterparts from the pragmatist camp. Yet there are reasons why continued negotiations are still important for U.S. policy. First, even if they yield few results, negotiations produce information and broaden America's contacts inside the regime, which may lead to unanticipated openings for influence and will undoubtedly yield a richer understanding of Iran's multipolar system. Second, even if broad agreement is impossible, negotiations can help reduce misunderstandings that can escalate into conflict.[28] Third, the process of talking can help de-mystify Iran, reducing the temptation to treat it as an aberrant actor in the international system that is somehow immune to the normal pressures and interests that inform state behavior. A peculiar form of mystique has defined the U.S. approach to Iran, one that defies America's history of engaging other international actors of varying shades of enmity and insalubrity. After all, the United States has talked to North Korea, Cuba, China, Somali warlords, Serbian paramilitaries, and even the Taliban.

Put differently, there is nothing uniquely exotic or risky about talking to Iranians. As with negotiators from other countries, Iranians expect each side to define the topic of the discussions, to articulate positions along with their attendant logic, and to agree on a common purpose or outcome. Fears of a culturally rooted Iranian preference for duplicity and dishonesty[29] are not only ethnocentric, but also unsupported by the testimonies of those who have negotiated with Iranians. That said, there do appear to be certain characteristics that shape

---

[28] For more on this outcome, particularly in the context of informal Track II negotiations, see Kaye, 2007.

[29] Such accusations are sometimes based on an orientalist and de-contextualized reading of the Shiite doctrine of *taqiyya* (dissimulation for self-preservation in the face of religious persecution).

the Iranian approach to negotiating, particularly in the context of the nuclear issue but also in business interactions.

The first of these characteristics is a tendency to revisit and reopen issues that both sides thought had been resolved. As noted by the Japanese expert:

> [B]e aware that even when the final accord has been reached, your Iranian counterpart may approach you seeking a last-minute renegotiation over the settled conditions in their favor. This may become frustrating and embarrassing to you, especially when you are in front of your company executives who have flown thousands of miles to ink the agreement. They might just want to make a good impression on their bosses, but the bottom line is that they are obsessed about being cheated and exploited by others.

Similarly, other observers have noted an Iranian tendency to defer the resolution of "weighty issues" and have recommended that any concessions to Iranian demands be seen as having been "earned" by the Iranians themselves. An Iranian-born analyst, reporting on his discussions with European Union (EU) negotiators, labeled these tendencies "confidence destroying" and compared the Iranian renegotiation of old agreements to "trying to sell a used rug twice." He also noted a myopic focus on maximizing short-term gains:

> The Iranians get wrapped up in subtle immediate details and miss out on strategic opportunities. They are like poker players in a chess game, constantly misjudging their own hand and focusing on tactical wins to the detriment of long-term strategy.

For further insights into the Iranian approach to negotiation, it is helpful to turn to some of the pioneering work on Iran by such social scientists as William Beeman, who authored a classic work on ta'arof[30]; James Bill, who conducted a study on social relations in Iran; and Marvin Zonis, who not only wrote on the Iranian political elite, but

---

[30] This important Persian cultural convention embodies exaggerated deference, politeness and self-deprecation.

also tried to discern popular attitudinal factors that resulted from and in turn helped influence Iranian culture and ultimately politics. All three of these scholars spent years living in Iran, are fluent in Persian, and did pioneering work that is still valid: Despite a change in political orientation and organization, Pahlavi Iran and the Islamic Republic of Iran are the same country. Zonis in particular has enumerated characteristics that define the pre-revolution elite and undoubtedly guide the contemporary Iranian approach to negotiation. These include political cynicism, personal mistrust, interpersonal exploitation, and manifest insecurity.[31]

Such generalizations, even if backed by rigorous field research and social science methodology, raise the larger and politically incorrect question of Iranian "national attributes." Here, it is helpful to turn to a decidedly nonacademic yet practical source—a manual written by a large Japanese corporation to prepare its businessman to negotiate in Iran. Business manuals can be especially useful guides, because they detach personal interactions from the ideologically induced tension that frequently obscures political discussions. In what is a very interesting analysis, the author of this Japanese manual, which we translated, sets out elements of the "Iranian psyche." Although somewhat stereotypical and reductionist, they are nonetheless worth considering:

- Individualistic
- Proud
- Value what's inside
- Hospitality
- Merchant at heart
- Artistic creativity
- Anti-establishment tendencies
- Victimization complex.

This last attribute raises the larger issue of whether the threat of force or force itself will spur Iran to negotiate and concede. Certainly, as we saw in May 2003, the credible threat of force is a powerful incen-

---

[31] Zonis, 1971, p. 11.

tive, but one that the United States has applied unevenly and unconvincingly against the Islamic Republic. In general, many in the Iranian leadership sense that they have been fortunate thus far in escaping the wrath that could follow U.S. exposure of Iranian misdeeds. Moreover, certain organs of the security establishment have vested institutional interests in maintaining a state of siege and keeping the country on a war footing—among its other benefits, this dynamic allows Iran to portray any domestic opponents as agents of foreign (read: U.S.) influence. How long certain segments of the population can endure this intensified crackdown on the allegedly U.S.-inspired "velvet revolution" remains to be seen, although the above-mentioned attribute of cynicism suggests an unusually high threshold for repression and misery as "business as usual."

Nonetheless, criticism appears to be rising among the political elite and even within Ahmadinejad's own power base that he has failed to take the U.S. threat seriously and that his rhetorical belligerence is leaving Iran increasingly beleaguered. If force were applied against the Islamic Republic, a popular uprising or a coup is unlikely but should not be dismissed outright. Probably, Persian nationalism and an impulse to "rally round the flag" will overshadow any previous criticisms of ill governance or diplomatic missteps by Ahmadinejad's coterie. Yet one must also consider the Islamic Republic's pronounced tradition of assigning blame, a tradition rooted in its factionalized structure and reaching back to the termination of the Iran-Iraq war, when then-President Rafsanjani quite explicitly condemned certain individuals' actions. Indeed, Rafsanjani recently emerged as one of the loudest voices for caution in the face of U.S. threats, invoking the authority of Khomeini and former IRGC commander Rezai in criticizing Ahmadinejad's obduracy on the nuclear issue as pushing the country toward war. In early October 2007, Rafsanjani disclosed the existence of a previously secret 1988 correspondence between Rezai and Khomeini in which Rezai warned that the Iran-Iraq war could not be won. With a single stroke, Rafsanjani effectively neutralized time-worn accusations that he alone was the sole proponent of the Iran-Iraq ceasefire, burnished his nationalist credentials, and showed that even the leader of the revolution was amenable to compromise if it secured the safety of the nation.[32]

---

[32] See Nafisi, 2006.

CHAPTER THREE

Conclusion: Iran Is Unlike Other Countries but Hardly Beyond Understanding

Our goal for this handbook was not to prescribe policy or to advocate, but to illuminate the deeper workings and processes of the Iranian system. The need for this illumination, apparent for some time, was made all the more apparent by the disclosure of the 2007 National Intelligence Estimate (NIE). In its revision of previous findings on Iran's nuclear *capabilities*, the NIE came to an important conclusion about Iranian *intentions* and *motivations* in positing that Iran halted its weaponization effort "primarily in response to increasing international scrutiny and pressure resulting from exposure of Iran's previously undeclared nuclear work."[1]

Over the years, there have been numerous attempts to locate the roots of Iran's intentions and motivations in the distinctiveness of its political culture and history. As a rich and ancient nation, Iran has always beguiled outside observers. Yet the complexity and diversity of daily life in Iran have always frustrated those eager to draw simple conclusions based on quick or superficial exposure to the country. This is clearly the case today for Americans who try to understand Iran at a distance—through the speeches of its leaders and the actions of its people taken in from thousands of miles away, at "listening posts" in Dubai, or at locations where expatriate Iranians may congregate, such as parts of Europe or the United States. Such mechanisms are cumulatively ineffective and indeed potentially dangerous. Certainly

---

[1] National Intelligence Council, 2007, p. 6.

the utterances of President Ahmadinejad and some of his equally blunt associates are attention getting. But the question is, particularly in light of the way in which power is distributed in Iran: How significant, representative, and even informative is this flamboyant rhetoric?

Our workshop sought to pierce the superficiality of previous policy analysis on Iran, challenging the notion of ideological uniformity within the regime and warning against a too-literal reading of Iranian politics. In canvassing the Iranian system, our participants highlighted a fierce cacophony within the factionalized decisionmaking apparatus, as well as a strong preference for consensus and for solicitation of public opinion that set it off markedly from other authoritarian regimes. Encompassing formal institutions, informal networks, and the associated personalities, Iran's political landscape is complex and multipolar; but it is not unfathomable, and it is hardly unique. Just like citizens in other states, Iranians are engaged in a dynamic set of debates about issues profound and mundane: sovereignty, identity, modernity, economic privilege, and political power. Ideology, brinksmanship, and anti-Americanism frequently make up the vocabulary of these deliberations but reveal little about their deeper meaning. Simply put, U.S. policymakers must avoid mistaking the terms of these debates for their substance.

De-mystification and understanding should therefore guide future U.S. approaches to the Islamic Republic. A successful U.S. strategy toward Iran may ultimately hinge on a more humble understanding of the country's complexity and a more sober recognition of its normalcy.

Workshop Agenda

An American Policymakers' Guide to
Understanding the Islamic Republic of Iran
Workshop Agenda
Organized by the RAND Corporation
October 29–30, 2007
Rome, Italy

	Monday, October 29	
9–11 a.m.	Introduction and welcome by Jerry Green and Charles Wolf	
	The Mechanics of Decisionmaking in Iran	
	Iran's Nuclear Program	Shahram Chubin
	Iran's Defense Establishment	Anoush Ehteshami
11–1 p.m.	Iran's Economy	
	Iran's Oil Sector: Puzzles and Explanations	Charles Wolf
	Economic Decisionmaking in Iran	Koichiro Tanaka
2–4 p.m.	Iran's Political Geography	
	Relations Between the Supreme Leader and the Sepah	Karim Sadjadpour
7:30	Dinner at Hotel Ponte Sisto	
	Tuesday, October 30	
9–11 a.m.	Mobilization and Dissent In and About Iran	
	The Politics of Factionalism in Iran	Amin Saikal
	Iran: Views from the Arab Gulf	Fred Wehrey
2–4 p.m.	Negotiating with Iran	
	Practical and Personal Experiences	Jim Dobbins
	The Art and Science of Negotiating with Iran	Jerry Green
	Wrap-up and conclusions by Jerry Green and Charles Wolf	

Workshop Papers

This appendix contains the papers written and presented by the workshop participants. We offer them here in the order of their presentation and in a state as close to the original as possible—in other words, they have been only lightly edited for minor elements of conformity and consistency (such as American English punctuation and spelling, and transliterations of Arab words and names). Our goal was to retain their authenticity in order for each author to speak in his own voice.

Decisionmaking for National Security: The Nuclear Case

By Shahram Chubin

Introduction

The nuclear issue has been compared to the oil nationalization case as a defining feature of modern Iran with comparable stakes and influence for Iran's future. The nature of decisionmaking on national security issues in Iran has tended to reflect the preference of the leadership to avoid public debate and to encourage citizen approval once a decision has been reached. The elements involved in reaching decisions, and specifically the nuclear case, is the subject of this short paper.

The topic is intrinsically a slippery one: National security inevitably is a sensitive subject, the more so when the stakes are so high. Decisions are thus made in secret, and information is only selectively leaked. To this is added the prevailing style of the IRI, which after thirty years in power still behaves like a revolutionary cabal rather than an established regime. Since the revolution, power in Iran has been decentralized, with several (competing) centers of power. This means that important decisions are rarely made without consultation or input from a variety of actors and sources. This is reflected in the government's mantra that Iranian decisions on the nuclear program reflect a "national consensus." This emphasis on "consensus" is convenient, for it allows the leadership to share the responsibility and the risks associated with a particular decision. It also serves to stifle disagreement on the grounds that a collective decision cannot brook subsequent criticism. The "national" consensus is in fact an "elite" consensus, and even this is an inaccurate characterization. What can be said is that the nuclear question *was* an elite issue until 2004–05, when the hard-line Majles and later Ahmadinejad decided to a make it a factional one. Populist trips and demagogic speeches took the issue from the elite to the broader public ("masses"), reducing the scope for flexibility by the leadership. A final note concerns the relationship between formal and informal decisionmaking. In Iranian culture, personal and family networks tend to function as alternatives as well as complements to formal links and institutional responsibilities. Thus, formal organo-grams only capture part of the dynamics of decisionmaking, as institutional relationships are only the visible part of the inputs on decisions.

Public Opinion and Decisionmaking

Public opinion is often invoked as a source of support for the nuclear program or a constraint preventing any deviation from it. Originally, when the nuclear program was restarted, in the mid-1980s, the public was not consulted. The later decision to seek enrichment was not publicly debated either. Iranian public opinion was neither a driver nor a constraint on the development of the program until 2002, when the full program, once exposed, became controversial. Until mid-2002, there was little discussion and no indication of a debate about the nuclear program, nuclear weapons, or current or future strategy.[1] There were complaints in 2003 that experts were being excluded from a rational discussion and that these were being submerged in a "security halo" with little reference to the economic feasibility of the proposed program.[2]

Public opinion is certainly a *background* factor in nuclear decisionmaking. Public dissatisfaction with the costs of the program or sanctions associated with it cannot be ignored either. Public opinion has been invoked as an important consideration by both factions:[3] as

---

[1] Writing earlier, I noted: "There is no debate in Iran about 'going nuclear' or about the place of nuclear weapons in current or future strategy." Doctrine was not discussed either. See "Does Iran Want Nuclear Weapons?" *Survival 1995*, Vol. 86, p. 99.

[2] "Iranian MP Proposes Nuclear Energy Plant Rethink," Yas-e Now Website, December 8, 2003, in *BBC Monitoring*, December 9, 2003. Nur Pir-Mozen, a Majles deputy and nuclear specialist observed that after many years and repeated questions about the technological situation and after the expenditure of millions of dollars, "We still do not know what has been going on in Bushire for the past thirty years." "Majles Deputy Questions Spending on Nuclear Power Plant," Mardom-Salari Website, Tehran, October 5, 2005, p. 11, in *BBC Monitoring*, October 7, 2005.

[3] It is my contention that, broadly, there are two factions on the nuclear issue: those that want to go ahead with enrichment at full speed whatever the cost and those that wish to obtain the technology without wrecking Iran's relations with the world or imposing a high cost on the country. These differences reflect broader ones on the necessity for seeking a nuclear capability versus a bomb and, more profoundly, whether Iran ought to become a normal state or continue to pursue its revolutionary agenda. This view is elaborated at greater length in my chapter "Iran: Domestic Politics and Nuclear Choices" in Michael Wills and

a reason for pursuing the program regardless by the hard-liners, and as a factor for caution by the pragmatists. The latter see the danger of pursuing a confrontational policy and its associated costs as likely to weaken the regime. In manipulating the issue, the regime is now more a captive of public opinion. Depending on the inclination, the conservatives, appealing to a largely fundamentalist constituency, see themselves constrained by public opinion from retreat; and the pragmatists (appealing to a more middle-class constituency) see the risks of a high-speed economic collision if the current course is pursued, with consequent damage to the regime. [4]

What is clear is that there has never been an informed debate about the energy rationale in the context of alternative policies and options. Nor has one been encouraged, least of all when the program was started. While most Iranians agree on Iran's right to seek modern technologies unrestricted, consensus clearly fades over the price Iranians are willing to pay for the continuation of the program in terms of sanctions, loss of confidence in investment, capital flight, and estrangement from the international community.[5]

Iranian politicians insist that there is a national consensus behind the nuclear program. This has given leverage to the negotiators and

Ashley Tellis (eds.), *Strategic Asia 2007/8*, Washington, D.C.: NBR, 2007. See also my *Iran's Nuclear Ambitions*, Washington, D.C.: Carnegie Endowment, 2006.

[4]   Chen Kane, "Nuclear Decision Making in Iran: A Rare Glimpse," *Middle East Brief No. 5*, Crown Center, Brandeis University, May 2006. The author notes how the negotiators under Rowhani, and by extension the leadership, were sensitive to public opinion on the nuclear issue: While supportive of Iran's "rights," they were very sensitive to the issue of the economic "costs."

[5]   See especially "Debating Iran's Nuclear Aspirations," pp. 104–107; Michael Herzog, "Iranian Public Opinion on the Nuclear Program," *Policy Focus No. 56*, Washington Institute, June 2006. See also Mahan Abdin, "Public Opinion and the Nuclear Standoff," *Mideast Mirror*, Vol. 1, No. 2, April/May 2006. A recent Zogby/Readers Digest poll reports that 41% of Iranians put reforming the economy before having a nuclear capability (27%). It also reveals a country divided on many issues (July 13, 2006: http://www.zogby.com/news/ReadNews.dbm?ID=1147). See also Mehdi Khalaj, "Ahmadinejad's Popularity One Year On," *Policy Watch No. 1125*, Washington Institute, July 20, 2006. A more recent poll reports that 84% of Iranians think it is very important for Iran to have a full fuel cycle, and 89% think it is very important for Iran to have a nuclear energy program (Common Ground/USIP Poll, January 16, 2007, World Public Opinion).

keeps sceptical politicians on board. In a system that has manipulated the issue of nuclear energy, depicting it as an issue of denial and discrimination, scepticism is in order when Iranian leaders insist that public opinion would or would not tolerate a certain path, or "forces them" to do such and such.[6]

Iran has argued its hands are tied by public opinion and the Majles. The government says it is under heavy pressure, with people and the media demanding results from the negotiations. This pressure stems from the hard-liners who shun any compromise and want to provoke an international crisis to strengthen their own grip on power.[7] Iranian negotiators use this pressure by in turn putting pressure on their European negotiating partners. The result is the kind of brinksmanship, a "managed crisis" just short of conflict, that characterized the negotiations from 2003 to 2005.[8]

At the same time it is clear that the regime itself manipulates the issue because the broad political context and climate necessarily affect decision-making. Hard-line newspapers such as *Keyhan,* that have quasi-official status, have more leeway than their dwindling reformist

---

[6] "Any Iranian government that wishes to stop uranium enrichment will fall." Rafsanjani: "They are telling us blatantly that we should not acquire nuclear technology: and we, in return, tell them that we shall not abandon the peoples' right and we shall not submit to bullying." "Iranian paper views delay to nuclear deal with Russia, "snub" to UK," Iran Website, Tehran, February 27, 2005, p. 2, in *BBC Monitoring,* February 28, 2005; Rafsanjani, "Ex-President Rafsanjani says Iran will not submit to bullying on nuclear issue," ISNA Website, Tehran, September 15, 2004, in *BBC Monitoring,* September 16, 2004. "One must accept that the nuclear file is one that is entirely national and ultimately related to the country's national security . . . ," "Iran press: Commentary Says Iran's Nuclear File 'National Challenge,'" Iran Website, Tehran, April 6, 2005, in *BBC Monitoring,* April 14, 2005.

[7] See Foreign Minister Kharrazi's comment on May 4, 2005, in Dafna Linzer, "Iran Says Nuclear Plans on Hold: Leaders Are Frustrated, but Still Hope for Progress in Talks," *The Washington Post,* May 5, 2005, p. A22; and the British diplomats' observation on how hard-line pressure translates into a tough rhetoric in the negotiations: Roger Wilkison, "EU Diplomats: Iran Risks Sanctions for Nuclear Activity," *Voice of America,* May 10, 2005, http://www.voanews.com/english/archive/2005-05/2005-05-10-voa34.cfm?CFID=46290374&CFTOKEN=56257987.

[8] See Gareth Smyth, "Nuclear Dispute Boosts Critics of 'Great Satan' in Iran Poll," *The Financial Times,* March 21, 2005, p. 7; and Gareth Smyth and Daniel Dombey, "EU3 Warns of 'managed crisis' over Iran Ambitions," *The Financial Times,* May 1, 2005.

counterparts in addressing the nuclear issue. This sets the tone for—and skews—the presentation of the issue.

Vested Interests and the Nuclear Program

The strongest supporters of the program, the Atomic Energy Organization (AEO) and the Revolutionary Guards (IRGC or Guards), reflect this. The AEO is concerned about the scientific/technical aspects of the program and the Guards with its security side. Both have vested interests in the program, though their interests are not identical or their political weight equal.

Iran envisages an ambitious nuclear energy program that includes about a dozen reactors generating about 10,000 MW.[9] The argument for energy diversification and self-sufficiency merges with that of scientific progress. Iran plans to be fully self-reliant in energy. This implies a program of "self sufficiency in all aspects of using the peaceful use of nuclear energy" from extraction through enrichment.[10]

Parallel to this is the growth of constituencies and bureaucracies that will benefit from such a program.[11] Iran's Atomic Energy Organization (AEO) is clearly an interested party in the program. It has furnished the technical input into a policy in which it has an enormous stake, supporting its ambitious scope.

---

[9] The figures vary between 7,000 and 10,000 MW and the reactors from ten to twenty. See the Iranian experts' discussion, "Iran Experts Say Nuclear Power Necessary for Electricity Generation," *Vision of the Islamic Republic of Iran Network 1*, June 13, 2004, in *BBC Monitoring*, June 14, 2004; The Chairman of the Majles Energy Committee, "Majlis Deputy Says Iran Needs Nine More Nuclear Power Plants," *Voice of the IRI*, October 25, 2004, in *BBC Monitoring*, October 26, 2004; and Majles National Security Committee Chairman Aladdin Borujerdi, who gives the number of power plants being considered at 20, "Iran Majlis Studying Proposals on Construction of 20 Nuclear Power Plants—MP," *Mehr News Agency*, January 30, 2005, in *BBC Monitoring*, February 1, 2005.

[10] Deputy Head of AEO Mohammad Saidi, "Nuclear Energy Top Priority in Iran's Nuclear Programme—Official," IRNA Website, March 22, 2005, in *BBC Monitoring*, March 23, 2005; and Elaine Sciolino, "Iran and the US Have One Thing in Common," *International Herald Tribune*, March 23, 2005, p. 4.

[11] For general comments along the same lines see Ray Takeyh, *Hidden Iran: Paradox and Power in the Islamic Republic*, New York: Henry Holt and Company, 2006, pp. 139–140, 154. He notes that some 250 scientists wrote letters urging the government not to cede its rights to technology (p. 156).

The opposition of the AEO to any freeze of enrichment stems in part from its impact on the retention and employment of scientific personnel.[12] The costs of a suspension, one expert argued, are a minimum loss of 5 billion U.S. dollars and the failure of fifteen years of effort. From a technical standpoint, the argument is that the elimination of one of the five phases of nuclear production "will render all other phases and the efforts of scientists in past years ineffective."[13]

Stopping centrifuges spinning and then restarting them is technically demanding for Iran at its current stage and will likely lead to crashes and costly delays to the program. Hence the AEO's opposition to suspension of enrichment. The AEO argues for an unconstrained program on security grounds as well: "If we do not produce nuclear fuel inside our country, they will use fuel as leverage to threaten our independence and territorial integrity in the future."[14] The Head of the AEO is a tireless promoter of the program, comparing the quest for indigenous enrichment with the need for food self-sufficiency. The AEO, not subject to political turnover, has a special clout within decisionmaking that comes from its consistent line and constant presence.[15]

The scope of Iran's ambitious nuclear program itself becomes an argument for its continuation. The opportunities for graft and payoffs in such expensive projects, not subject to normal auditing, are an additional incentive. Most analysts believe that the IRGC is the strongest

---

[12] On the costs of suspension and technical problems caused, see the AEO head, Aghazadeh, "Iran's Atomic Energy Chief Says Suspension of Uranium Enrichment Problematic," ISNA Website, Tehran, December 12, 2003, in *BBC Monitoring*, December 12, 2003. On the retention of personnel indispensable for further progress in the nuclear area, see Aghazadeh, "Iranian Officials Discuss Ways to Retain Nuclear Scientists," Shargh Website, Tehran, December 16, 2004, in *BBC Monitoring*, December 20, 2004.

[13] See the discussion of the nuclear expert, "Cessation of Iran's Enrichment Programme Not an Option—Agency," Baztab Website, March 30, 2005, in *BBC Monitoring*, April 1, 2005.

[14] AEO Deputy Director Mohammad Sai'di, *Mehr* news agency, in English, January 17, 2007, in *BBC Monitoring*, January 18, 2007.

[15] See especially Gholam Reza Aghazadeh, ISNA Website, March 7, 2007, in *BBC Monitoring*, March 8, 2007. For the continuity of AEO in decisionmaking, see Aghazadeh, ISNA Website, April 17, 2007, in *BBC Monitoring*, April 18, 2007.

lobby for a nuclear option.[16] Tasked formally with the defense of the revolution (as opposed to territorial or national defense), the IRGC has been put in charge of the missile force and nuclear installations. Yet its accountability and mission remain opaque. In the past it has interfered politically and appears to have organized itself politically. Its security role has been eclipsed by its commercial activities. Together with its affiliates, it has spread itself in the economy, winning over $5 billion (U.S. dollars) in no-bid contracts from the government.[17] These unusual commercial activities are paralleled by black market smuggling of (subsidized) oil for export for profit and other questionably legal activities.[18]

The increasing role of the Revolutionary Guards in Iran's politics is another source of concern. Of 152 new members elected to the Majles in February 2004, 91 had Guards backgrounds, while a further 34 former Guards officers now hold senior-level posts in the government.[19] In the June 2005 presidential elections, besides Ahmadinejad, there were three other candidates from the Guards. The dominance of the Guards and Intelligence officials could open the country to a new militarism.[20] The Guards has taken on aspects of a "state within a state" answerable to no one and acting unilaterally on issues where its interests are concerned.[21] This apparent carte blanche to act where

---

[16] E.g., Ray Takeyh, "Understanding the Iran Crisis," testimony before the U.S. House Committee on Foreign Affairs, Washington D.C., January 31, 2007. (Takeyh adds the conservative Guardians Council as another supporter.) See also Takeyh, *Hidden Iran*, p. 157.

[17] "Iran: Ahmadi-Nejad's Tumultuous Presidency," ICG Report, Middle East Briefing No. 21, February 6, 2007, pp. 12–14.

[18] Milani testimony, the U.S. House Foreign Relations Committee, Washington D.C., January 31, 2007, pp. 8–9.

[19] Quoted in Judith Yaphe and Charles Lutes, "Reassessing the Implications of a Nuclear Iran," McNair Paper No. 69, Washington, D.C: National Defence University, 2005, p. 6.

[20] See Bill Sami'i, "The Military-Mullah Complex: The Militarization of Iranian Politics," *The Weekly Standard*, May 14, 2005; and Mohsen Sazegara, "The New Iranian Government: Resurrecting Past Errors," *Policy Watch No. 1013*, Washington Institute for Near East Policy, July 2005.

[21] Notably, in parading captured British troops that allegedly strayed into Iranian territory in mid-2004 in a provocative manner, blindfolded, reminiscent of the U.S. embassy

it chooses amounts to a veto power forcing the government to negotiate with the IRGC to find a solution.[22] The insulation of the IRGC
from government control, its autonomy in action, makes it difficult
to know when a particular activity reflects the "decentralized way in
which power" works in Iran, or is, in fact, an extension of the government's policy. Attribution of responsibility for the activities of the Qods
Brigade of IRGC in Iraq to the Iranian leadership has been difficult,
given this situation.[23] Recent IRGC behavior suggests that it is not
"afraid of provoking a crisis." This was illustrated in February 2007,
during the deployment of U.S. carriers to the Persian Gulf. IRGC elements were reported to have secretly painted their emblem on the side
of a U.S. warship, a risky act at best.[24] And again, in March, when they
took prisoner 15 British sailors later released.[25]

In light of the growing and spreading influence of the IRGC
politically and economically, with commercial as well as security interests, it is clear that it is a formidable interest group.[26] As the IRGC has

---

hostages; and later, the closure of a new airport that the IRGC believed should not be under
contract to a Turkish company (that might have ties with Israel).

[22] Ali M. Ansari, *Confronting Iran*, New York: Basic Books, 2006, pp. 218–220.

[23] Ansari, *Confronting Iran*, p. 220. On Iraq, note President Bush, referring to the Iranian
leadership and the Qods brigade in Iraq: "What's worse—that the government knew or that
the government didn't know?" Brian Knowlton, "Bush Keeps Pressure on Iran Over Arms,"
International Herald Tribune, February 16, 2007, p. 1/8.

[24] The phrase is Ansari's (2006). See the report in *Keyhan*, February 14, 2007, based on
Shushtari, commander of the ground forces of the IRGC, *BBC Monitoring*, February 15,
2007.

[25] The most plausible explanation for this episode (beside retaliation for U.S. arrests of revolutionary guards in Iraq) was that it was political diversion for a regime that recognizes its
unpopularity. See Juan Cole, "Iran's New Hostage Crisis," April 3, 2007, http://www.salon.
com/opinion/feature/2007/04/03/iran/.

[26] This commercial interest also makes the IRGC reluctant to a normalization of relations
with the West. See interview of Karim Sajjadpour, "Revolutionary Guards Have Financial
Interest in keeping Iran isolated," *The New York Times*, August 6, 2007 (available as of August
27, 2008 at http://www.nytimes.com/cfr/world/slot1_20070529.html?pagewanted=print).
For an informed and critical view of the evolution of the guards, see Mohsen Sazegara, "What
Was Once a Revolutionary Guard is Now Just a Mafia," *Forward*, March 16, 2007 (available
as of August 27, 2008 at http://www.forward.com/articles/what-was-once-a-revolutionary-
guard-is-now-just-a/).

taken on the characteristics of a state within a state, there appear to be few obstacles to the realization of its aims.

Since we do not have access to a debate about nuclear *weapons* within the leadership itself, we are left to conjecture about the role of the Guards in such a debate. We do know that as the custodian of the related technology (missiles), the Guards is supportive of technologies that are equalizers or shortcuts militarily. During the last phase of the war with Iraq, Guards Commander Mohsen Rezai argued that without nuclear weapons, Iran could not continue the war with any hope of winning.[27] Except for expressing scepticism about arms control agreements, the IRGC has not publicly expressed an institutional view about nuclear weapons as such. Like most of the hard-liners in the regime, the IRGC has supported the nuclear program. In private and in the SNSC, it may be expected to take a strong position in favor of pressing on with the nuclear program with the minimum of constraints.

The nuclear option, more than any other, "directly addresses their corporate needs and strategic outlook." It is an outgrowth of the IRGC's experience in the Iran-Iraq war with missiles and chemical weapons. With missiles (which are under IRGC control), a nuclear option could deter attacks on Iran and project power (or influence) regionally, and, not least, it reinforces the IRGC role vis-à-vis the larger regular armed forces.[28]

Nuclear Decisionmaking

Major national security issues are decided in the Supreme National Security Council (SNSC), which includes the President, the Defense and Foreign Ministers, the Commander of the Revolutionary Guards, and several appointees or "representatives" of the Supreme Guide. This

---

[27] For a useful and accessible summary of this episode, see Najmeh Bozorghmehr, "Nuclear Row Sparks Echoes of Iran's Brutal War with Iraq," *The Financial Times*, October 26, 2006, p. 5. See also Rasool Nafisi, "The Khomeini Letter: Is Rafsanjani Warning the Hardliners?" The author notes that the incident "reveals the diversity of views on the nuclear issue." Iranian.com, October 11, 2006 (available as of August 24, 2008 at http://www.iranian.com/RasoolNafisi/2006/October/Nuclear/index.html).

[28] Ali Gheissari and Vali Nasr, "The Conservative Consolidation in Iran," *Survival*, Vol. 47, No. 2, 2005, pp. 177, 179, 188.

council is broadly reflective of the elite. The Secretary of the SNSC (Ali Larijani replaced Hasan Rowhani in 2005) is broadly the equivalent of the U.S. National Security Adviser. The attached chart schematically and approximately reflects the nuclear decisionmaking structure. In addition to the chart, one should note the Supreme Leader's "soundings" among his clerical network (in Qom and elsewhere) and the primacy of informal networks. The Supreme Guide has special representatives in the SNSC (Rowhani) and special advisers on Foreign Affairs (former Foreign Minister Akbar Velayati) and for military affairs (former Guards Commander Rahim Safavi). All of these former officials and others are likely to be consulted by him when they do not participate in important sessions of the SNSC.

Among the inputs into decisions are interested parties such as the Atomic Energy Organisation, which looks to its institutional interests and is a strong supporter of the nuclear program. It can make inputs on the technical side, point to the valuable experience acquired, and underscore the costs of a long suspension of activities in terms of morale and attrition of scientific personnel. The Foreign Ministry and SNSC Secretary can argue the costs of estrangement and confrontation with Europe and the IAEA, and point to international obligations and fashion a diplomatic strategy. Reflecting the principal political tendencies, the appointment of Hasan Rowhani, the long-standing secretary and pragmatist as chief nuclear negotiator in 2003, was in itself a significant choice. With the arrival of a more conservative and hard-line government in August 2005, the composition of the leadership of the SNSC accordingly changed, notably the Foreign and Defense ministers and the secretary of the SNSC.

The formal and informal structures allow broad consultation expressed in "consensus." The "consensus" in fact is a form of self-protection for the elite, implying *collective decisionmaking and responsibility*. Thus, once a decision has been made, the elite are all in it together, with little room for opting out or exploiting mistakes or setbacks. This serves as a safety net on especially contentious questions, such as freezing or reversing course on the nuclear program. At the same time, the consensus, however illusory, is an insurance policy against foreign exploitation of internal differences.

The Supreme Guide, who has the final word, is prone to balancing factional demands. As "arbiter" it is unclear whether he follows or forms the prevailing consensus, though he is clearly more comfortable with hard-liners. Indeed, the default position on national security issues has been and remains hard-line. (Contrast Khamenei's fulsome praise and indulgence of Ahmadinejad with the manner in which Khatami was marginalized on national security issues.) Khamenei's preferences and temporizing have stamped incoherence on Iran's foreign and security policies.[29] In defining and hyping the importance of the nuclear issue, a populist president has largely outmaneuvered and upstaged the Supreme Guide.[30] This, together with the technical inertia behind the nuclear program, means that the program's reversal or freeze will be more difficult politically, requiring a kind of decisionmaking alien to the characteristically indecisive Khamenei.[31]

Conclusion

Decisionmaking on the nuclear issue is similar to that on all national security issues, through the SNSC complemented by consultation with others: former officials, confidantes, and technicians. Conceived in secrecy in a limited circle, the program became more public after 2002–03. As the stakes increased, the regime found it politic to widen the circle, though public information was limited and debate was discouraged. Decisionmaking now is said to reflect a consensus, a position intended to cover the very different views of the two principal groups on the wisdom of pressing the nuclear issue to the exclusion of other, more practical questions facing the IRI. On the nuclear issue, two groups with vested interests, the AEO and the IRGC, have been

---

[29] "The real government of Iran, the one controlled by Khamenei, sees its future in stable authoritarianism." Ali Gheissari and Vali Nasr, "The Conservative Consolidation in Iran," *Survival*, Vol. 47, No. 2, 2005, p. 176.

[30] See "Whither Iran?" and Bernard Hourcade, "Iran's Internal Security Challenges," in W. Posch (ed.), "Iranian Challenges," *Chaillot Paper 89*, Paris: Institute for Security Studies, 2006, p. 57.

[31] See Marie Claude Decamps, "L'Iran Veut Negocier sur la Dossier Nucleaire sans Perdre la Face," *Le Monde*, March 9, 2007, p. 1. (Without Khamenei pronouncing on the subject, the nuclear issue is a tug of war between the factions.)

(more than probably) disproportionately influential. This together with the Supreme Guide's preference for a hard line on foreign policy, which gives the regime the sense of embattlement that justifies it, accounts for the race for enrichment. The closer Iran gets to mastering enrichment (3,000 centrifuges spinning continuously for one year), the more difficult it will be to argue for a freeze or suspension. The technical and political momentum at work will thus need decisive leadership to be arrested. Only if the regime senses a real threat is that type of leadership likely to be forthcoming.

Appendix: Illustrative, Not Exhaustive, List of Decisionmaking Figures.[32]

Hasan Rowhani, former Secretary of SNSC and chief nuclear negotiator, currently the Supreme Leader's representative to SNSC and Director of Strategic Centre attached to the Expediency Council.

Ali Larijani, formerly in charge of Radio and Television, now Secretary of SNSC and chief nuclear negotiator. (Ran for office as President, 2005.)

Hossein Moussavian, formerly Ambassador to Germany, and deputy to Rowhani at the SNSC and deputy nuclear negotiator, and now deputy at the Expediency Council's Strategic Centre.

Hashemi Rafsanjani, former President, assigned by Khomeini as Head of Armed Forces (1988–89), heads Expediency Council and more recently the Assembly of Experts.

Mohammed Khatami, former President, now in charge of Dialogue of Civilisations foundation.

Mohsen Rezai, former IRGC Commander, now Secretary of the Expediency Council.

Ali Akbar Velayati, former longtime Foreign Minister and now foreign affairs advisor to the Supreme Guide.

Yahya Rahim Safavi, former Guards commander, now senior advisor on the armed forces to the Supreme Guide.

---

[32] Indicative of tendency to include all major officials and to have them play overlapping roles to balance each other.

Mohammad Ali Jafari, former IRGC commander of land forces, now Commander of the IRGC.

Ali Shamkhani, Admiral, former Defense Minister, now Military Adviser to the Supreme Guide.

Mohammad Najjar, current Defense Minister.

Bager Zolgadr, former head of IRGC land forces, now Interior Ministry.

Ala'eddin Borujerdi, Head of the Majlis National Security and Foreign Affairs Policy Committee.

Abdol Reza Rahmani Fazli, deputy to the Secretary of the SNSC.

Javad Vai'idi, Deputy Secretary of the SNSC.

Mohammad Sai'idi, Deputy Secretary of the SNSC for International Affairs.

Hoseyn Shariatmadari, Editor of Keyhan and special representative of the Supreme Guide.

Kamal Kharrazi, former Foreign Minister and now Chairman of the Strategic Council for Foreign Policy.

Actual and former heads of the Atomic Energy Organization, such as Aghazadeh.

Nuclear Decisionmaking: The Formal Structure

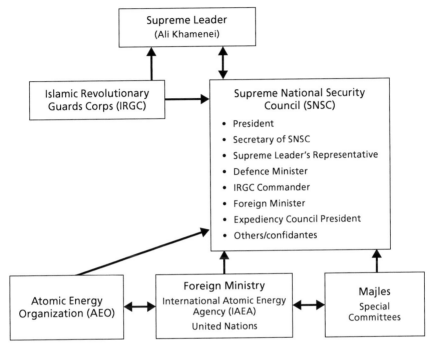

RAND *MG771-AppB*

Negotiating with Iran: A Case Study

By James Dobbins

There is a popular perception in the United States that in the aftermath of 9/11, the United States formed a coalition and overthrew the Taliban. Wrong. In the aftermath of 9/11, the United States joined an existing coalition that had been trying to overthrow the Taliban for much of a decade. The coalition consisted of India, Russia, Iran, and the Northern Alliance. And with the addition of American airpower, that coalition succeeded in ousting the Taliban.

The success in quickly forming a successor regime was also thanks to this coalition. As the American representative to the Afghan opposition, I represented the United States at the Bonn conference that met for that purpose. The conference had representation from all of the major elements of the Afghan opposition and from all of the principal regional states—the countries that had been playing the great game and tearing Afghanistan apart for 20 years—Russia, India, Pakistan, Iran, and of course the United States.

At one point, the UN had circulated the first draft of the Bonn declaration, which is essentially Afghanistan's interim constitution. It was the Iranian envoy who noted that there was no mention of democracy. "Maybe a document like this ought to mention democracy," he suggested. I allowed as how that was probably a good idea. I have to note that my instructions didn't say anything about democracy. We weren't on a democracy campaign at that stage. We wanted a government that would work with us to track down remaining al-Qaeda elements, and we sought to construct a broadly based, representative government that could keep the country in peace.

It was also the Iranian delegation that proposed that the document should commit the Afghans to cooperate against international terrorism.

At one point, I reproached my Iranian colleague, Deputy Foreign Minister Javad Zarif, because his foreign minister had been quoted the day before as saying that he didn't think any peacekeeping troops were necessary for Kabul. I said to my Iranian colleague, "Well you and I have agreed that we really need a peacekeeping force in Kabul. Why is your foreign minister being quoted to the contrary?"

"You can consider my Minister's statement a gesture of solidarity with Don Rumsfeld," Zarif replied with a grin. "After all, Jim, you and I are both way out in front of our instructions on this one, aren't we?" I had to admit this was true.

On the last night of the conference we'd agreed on everything except who was going to govern Afghanistan. We had the interim constitution, but we were still arguing about who was going to govern Afghanistan. The Northern Alliance was insisting upon occupying 18 of the 26 ministries, and everyone else agreed that was too many. It wasn't going to be broadly based if the Northern Alliance, which represented maybe 30 or 40% of the population, got 75% of the ministries.

And so at my suggestion, Lakhdar Brahimi, the UN negotiator, got together all of the foreign ambassadors who were still awake—it was about 2 in the morning—which was a kind of self-selective process. If they were still awake, they cared a lot. And so it consisted of me, the Iranian, the Russian, the Indian, and the German (our host). For two hours we worked over the Northern Alliance representative, Younnis Qanooni, each of us arguing, in turn, that he should agree to give up several ministries. He remained obdurate. Finally, Zarif took him aside and whispered to him for a few moments, following which the Northern Alliance envoy returned to the table and said, "Okay, I agree. The other factions can have two more ministries. And we can create three more, which they can also have." We had a deal. Afghanistan would be governed by twenty-nine Cabinet-level officials, too many for any state, but the result was balanced and the conference could conclude.

Four hours later, the German Chancellor arrived and the Bonn agreement was signed. And that was how the final breakthrough in the negotiation was achieved.

Iran had the most senior delegation to Karzai's inauguration. Their foreign minister came. There had been some doubt about whether Ismail Khan, a warlord in the area closest to Iran, was going to support this settlement. The Iranian foreign minister landed in Herat, picked Khan up, put him on the plane, and brought him to Kabul just to make sure no one doubted that he was going to support the conclusion.

In the Tokyo donors conference that came a few weeks later, Iran pledged $500 million in assistance to Afghanistan, assistance which by and large it has since delivered, which is a staggering amount for a non-first-world country and was by far the largest of any of the non-OECD countries at the pledges. The American pledge, by comparison, was all of $290 million, little more than half that of Iran.

Several of the Iranian diplomats who had been in Bonn were with us again in Tokyo. Emerging from a larger gathering, one of them took me aside to reaffirm his government's desire to continue to cooperate on Afghanistan. I agreed that this would be desirable but warned that Iranian behavior in other areas represented an obstacle to cooperation.

"We would like to discuss the other issues with you also," he replied.

"My brief only extends to Afghanistan," I cautioned.

"We know that. We would like to work on these other issues with the appropriate people in your government."

"The Karine A incident was not helpful," I said, referring to a Palestinian ship intercepted a few days earlier by the Israeli Navy on its way to Gaza loaded with several tons of Iranian-origin weapons.

"We too are concerned about this," my Iranian interlocutor said. "President Khatemi met earlier this week with the National Security Council. He asked whether any of the agency representatives present knew anything about this shipment. All of them denied any knowledge of it. If your government has any information to the contrary it can provide us, that would be most helpful."

Treasury Secretary Paul O'Neill, also in Tokyo for the donors meeting, had a similar approach from a senior United Nations official delivering a message from the Iranian regime. His interlocutor was Mrs. Sadako Ogata, the United Nations High Commissioner for Refugees. She had asked to see him in order to pass on a message from the Iranian government. Ogata told O'Neil that the Iranians wanted to open a dialogue with Washington covering all of the issues that divided the two countries.

On returning to Washington, O'Neill and I reported these conversations, he to Rice and his Cabinet-level colleagues, I to State's Middle Eastern Bureau. No one expressed any interest in following up these openings. One week later, in a State of the Union address, President Bush included Iran, along with its arch enemy, Iraq, in what he termed an "axis of evil," implicitly threatening both states, along with North Korea, with preemptive military action intended to halt their acquisition of weapons of mass destruction.

Two months thereafter, the Iranians asked to see me on the fringes of another multilateral meeting we were having about Afghanistan in Geneva. They introduced me to the Iranian general who had been the commander of their security assistance efforts for the Northern Alliance throughout the war. And he said, "We're prepared to house, pay, clothe, arm, and train up to 20,000 troops in a broader program under American leadership."

So I said, "Well, if you train some Afghan troops and we train some, they'd end up having a different doctrine."

The general just laughed, and he said, "Don't worry, we're still using the manuals you left behind in 1979."

So I said, "Okay, so maybe they might have compatible doctrines, but they might have conflicting loyalties."

And he said, "Well, we trained, we equipped, and, by the way, we're the ones who are still paying for the Afghan troops you're still using in the southern part of the country to go after Taliban and Al Qaeda elements. Are you having any difficulty with their loyalty?"

"No, not that I know of," I admitted. I said I'd go back and report that to Washington.

This unexpected offer struck me as problematic in detail but promising in its overall implications. Despite the general's assurances, I could foresee problems in having Iran and the United States training different components of a new Afghan army. On the other hand, Iranian participation, under American leadership, in a joint program of this sort would be a breathtaking departure after more than twenty years of mutual hostility. It also represented a significant step beyond the quiet diplomatic cooperation we had achieved so far. Clearly, despite having been relegated by President Bush to the "axis of evil" two months earlier, the Khatemi government wanted to deepen its cooperation with Washington.

Back home, I immediately went to see Powell.

"Very interesting," he responded to my account of this conversation. "You need to brief Condi."

And so I went to see Rice.

"Very interesting," she said. "You need to talk to Don."

Several days later, Rice called a meeting of NSC Principals to discuss the Iranian offer, among other matters. When we came to that item on the agenda, I again recounted my conversation with the Iranians. Rumsfeld did not look up from the papers he was perusing throughout my presentation. When I finished, he made no comment and asked no questions. Neither did anyone else. After a brief pause, seeing no one ready to take up the issue, Rice moved the meeting on to the next item on her agenda. Insofar as I am aware, the issue was never again discussed. The Iranians never received a response.

Iran's Defense Establishment

By Anoush Ehteshami

Introduction

Despite the general difficulties encountered in trying to understand the complexities and inter-institutional workings of the Iranian state, it is not impossible to get a good sense of the Iranian defense establishment in terms of its structures and place in the nezam (the governing system of the IRI). In personnel terms, the defense establishment is approximately 550,000 strong, with the army forming the largest single force (350,000) and the Sepah (Islamic Revolutionary Guards Corps—Sepah-e Pasdaran-e Enghelab-e Islami) the second largest with 125,000 personnel. But size is not an accurate indication of role and influence, for the IRGC is in fact by far the most important military organization in the country today, with its own defense college, think tank, military production and commercial arms, and of course political clout.

Evolution of the Defense Establishment

The armed forces (Artesh) and the Sepah are accountable to Supreme Leader Ayatollah Ali Khamenei as their commander-in-chief. During Rafsanjani's first administration (1989–1993), the Artesh's position was reestablished as the defender of the country's territorial integrity, and the Sepah was encouraged to embrace a single administrative structure with the Artesh as its backbone. Management lines were reformed and simplified, and the newly established Supreme National Security Council was given the all-important task of threat assessment and evaluation. Toward the end of his first term and throughout the second, however, Rafsanjani was hampered by the activities of a resurgent (New) Right, which had capitalized on the demise of the left-centrist forces at the hands of Rafsanjani to build a powerful institutional base across the governing framework; they found a strong foothold in the Leader's office, the Majles, the judiciary, the Intelligence Ministry, and the Sepah. Several Sepah and Basij leaders openly attached their colors to the Right's mast at the time and supported the candidacy of Hojjatoleslam Nateq-Nouri, who until then had been Speaker of Parliament.

In other areas too, the 1990s brought many uncertainties for Iranians. Changes in different stratas' social and economic positions followed the introduction of privatization, which hit some of the elite's vested interests while enriching others. And multiple exchange rates, which were abolished in Khatami's second term, adversely affected the bazaar and money-changing communities. In a nutshell, Rafsanjani's economic initiatives destabilized the social pyramid sufficiently for serious tensions to begin to appear in the edifice of the republic, particularly in relations between the state and civil society. These tensions began manifesting themselves in different ways: riots, strikes and sit-ins, political protests. They had at their core, however, problems associated with major changes in the Islamic state's responsibilities toward the "deprived," its policies with regard to distribution of wealth and income, and the concentration of economic power in the hands of the regime's associates and inner core—all issues that Ahmadinejad built his 2005 presidential campaign around.

Such tensions in turn slowly raised questions about the place of the military as a sociopolitical force in the new social environment. After 1997, moreover, when factionalist politics escalated to the point of violence, it not only embroiled elements from the Pasdaran, but also posed serious challenges for the national security forces, whose primary function is to keep order. But the question remained, Should they try to keep order, or do they step out of the way of legitimate demonstrations for reform? For the Sepah, in particular, the question was whether it should feel that the regime in its entirety was under threat, should legitimately deploy its forces "in defense of the revolution," which it has the constitutional responsibility to do under Article 150 of the Constitution. While during the Rafsanjani period the clarity of mission of the various military commands was not tested, during Khatami's presidency this problem emerged as one of the single most important issues affecting civil-military relations—the tone for which was already being set by the open support that General Mohsen Rezai, Commander of the Sepah for 16 years, was providing for the conservative candidate in May 1997's presidential race. General Rezai also placed the explanation for the actions of the Sepah leadership during the election campaign in a much broader context. As he stated soon after the election of the new president in 1997: "It is very difficult for the IRGC men who obey the instructions of the Vali [Leader] to see that there are persons among the associates of the president-elect who question the concept of absolute guardianship of the Vali-ye Faqih and even dare to consider the vote of the people above that of the Leader. In the meantime, Iran is the land of the 'Imam of the Time' and speaking about national sovereignty and man-made laws vis-à-vis the Divine laws, had made the dear Islamic Guards seriously concerned."[33]

Role of the Defense Establishment in the Political Process

The failure to achieve Islamic social justice and welfare for the poor (mostazafin) was exemplified in the Rafsanjani administration's economic liberalization strategy. This produced a backlash at both the mass and the elite level. The liberalization strategy led to urban riots and a more direct involvement of the reconstituted security forces in domestic affairs. At the elite level, the failures of the Islamic justice program generated new demands, largely from the neoconservative factions, for the imposition of stricter cultural norms. This was not an unnatural response to the realities of life in the Islamic Republic of Iran, in which all that remained of the distinction between Islamic Iran and its predecessor was in the cultural realm.

The New Right movement, which first made its organized presence felt in 1993 (after that year's presidential elections), accelerated the pace of its political march in the mid-1990s, and from March 1996 it openly began challenging the pragmatists' grip on power. It did much, in the Majles and elsewhere, to weaken the Rafsanjani administration's institutional control and its public policy reforms. For a while, the stunning defeat of the New Right's champion (Hojjatoleslam Nateq-Nouri) in the May 1997 presidential elections did help to check their

---

[33] The interview was apparently given to *al-Hayat* but received wide coverage in Iran itself. See *Ettala'at*, June 23, 1997. Rezai relinquished his position as Commander of the Sepah in September 1997 and soon joined the Expediency Council under the chairmanship of the former President Rafsanjani.

growing influence. But due to the disparate nature of Khatami's coalition, the ideological and political divisions in the ranks of his allies, and, perhaps most important of all, the entrenched position that the New Right has had in the key institutions of power, neoconservatism remained a potent force. For all the public support he enjoyed, it proved very difficult for President Khatami to decisively reverse the balance of power in favor of his own camp. This was driven home in February 2004's elections for the Seventh Majles. Through manipulation of the candidates' list by the conservative-dominated Council of Guardians, the reformers decisively lost control of the Majles and also ensured that a high proportion of deputies with links to the Sepah or related organizations were to be present in the new Majles.[34]

When the Iranian political system is settled down to the drum of regular, openly contested elections, it seems easier for the Artesh and the Sepah to stay out of domestic squabbles of the political elite and not compromise their political presence. But when the system itself generates instability and when elections result in the rise of a "Third Force"[35-ᴬ] —a new and different revolutionary agenda—it is far from clear that the Sepah (and its associates at least) will be disinclined to act as independent actors.

Many centers of power are present in Iran evolving around religious, political, economic, and military figures. The IRGC and the security forces have emerged as the most independent power and prevail over all others centers of power in Iran.[36] The U.S. military threats against Iran, nuclear confrontation with the West, and the invasion of Iraq are among the fundamental causes behind this gain in power. Today, a group associated with the Sepah controls the major state-sponsored media. After gaining control of numerous city and town councils in 2003, many former members of the IRGC or its associates

---

[34] It has been suggested that as many as 90 of the 290 deputies in the Seventh Majles have an IRGC or military background.

[35] This notion has been borrowed from J. Amuzegar. See "Iran's Crumbling Revolution," *Foreign Affairs*, Vol. 82, No. 1, January/February 2003, pp. 44–57.

[36] "Iran's Revolutionary Guards making a bid for increased power," *Euro Asia Insight*, May 19, 2004.

managed to enter into the legislative branch in the 2004 elections. The group had also set its sights on gaining control of the executive branch in the 2005 presidential elections. In these presidential elections, out of 1,010 candidates, the Guardian Council confirmed only six individuals as qualified candidates to participate and contest the elections. Of the six qualified to stand, four were in fact former IRGC commanders and two were clerics.[37] Prior to taking on a higher political profile, the IRGC established itself as an economic force in the country, controlling a vast array of financial and economic enterprises. In large part, the businesses were seen as needed to finance Revolutionary Guards security programs. At the same time, the ventures were intended to build the Sepah's independence. In this, Sepah commanders sought to mimic their military counterparts in Pakistan and Turkey.[38] In both those countries, the army has tended to act as far more than an instrument to protect national interests: In both, the army has a high-profile political role and often defines the nation's security interests.

Since 1997, the Sepah in Iran has had a growing influence on foreign policy, strategic thinking, and the economy.[39] This "Praetorian Guard" has been a cornerstone of the conservatives' survival and comeback strategy since 1997 and has been substantially rewarded by Khamenei. The IRGC has a strong presence on the Supreme National Security Council. Signs of the ever-growing political clout of the Revolutionary Guards are abundant. For instance, on May 18, 2004, a former Sepah commander, Ezzatolah Zarghami, was named to the key post of national television and radio chief. In addition, in apparent exchange for its help during the parliamentary elections, the IRGC was permitted to field its own slate of candidates. Thus, when the new parliament convened later in May, about a dozen legislators were under the effective control of the Revolutionary Guards. This is the first time in the Islamic Republic's history that the Sepah has had such a parliamentary presence. By far the greatest demonstration of the Revolution-

---

[37] "The military-mullah complex; the militarization of Iranian politics," *Weekly Standard*, May 23, 2005.

[38] *Euro Asia Insight*, May 19, 2004.

[39] *Euro Asia Insight*, May 19, 2004.

ary Guards' political influence occurred in early May 2004, when the military abruptly closed down Tehran's new Imam Khomeini International Airport.[40] In justifying its action, the Guards representatives said the fact that a Turkish consortium, TAV, was in charge of operating the airport terminal posed a threat to Iran's "security and dignity," according to the IRNA. Accordingly, the Sepah demanded that the TAV airport deal be voided before the airport reopens. Some observers suspected that an economic motive was behind the Revolutionary Guards action in the airport row. When TAV won the tender to operate the airport, the losing bidder was reportedly a company with close ties to the Revolutionary Guards.[41]

The IRGC's influence has remained: The main candidates of the IRGC in the 2005 presidential elections were Ali Larijani, a former IRGC commander and the ex-director of the highly politicized state television and radio network, and Mohammad Baqer Qalibaf, the former chief of Tehran's police force, who is also a former IRGC commander. Qalibaf openly declared himself to be a "religiously" devout Reza Shah.[42] Qalibaf noted that Iranians were tired of the country's chaotic power relations and were desperate for central rule. Mohsen Rezai, a longtime commander-in-chief of the IRGC and the speaker of the Expediency Council, was another military-oriented candidate.

If further sign of the militarization of the political space in Iran were needed, it would be the fact that 10 of Dr. Ahmadinejad's cabinet nominees have had military or security backgrounds.[43] The militarization of Iranian politics has drawn strong criticism from the reformist camp. For example, reformist presidential candidate Mehdi Karrubi stated in a late March meeting with officials from his election headquarters that in recent years he has been warning of the IRGC involvement in political affairs. The daily *Etemad* quoted him as saying: "I

---

[40] *Euro Asia Insight,* May 19, 2004.

[41] *Euro Asia Insight,* May 19, 2004.

[42] K. Alamdari, "The power structure of the Islamic Republic of Iran: Transition from populism to clientelism and militarization of the government," *Third World Quarterly,* Vol. 26, No. 8, 2005, pp. 1285–1301.

[43] *Emrooz,* August 16, 2005, at http://www.emrouz.info/Showitem.aspx? ID=4900&p=1.

have repeatedly condemned it and have openly criticized them."[44] He added that it is a mistake to ignore the actions of the IRGC, the Basij, the Guardians Council, the judiciary, the Special Court for the Clergy, and agencies affiliated with the Supreme Leader in the 2005 presidential elections. Mehdi Karrubi and Mostafa Moin claimed that Ahmadinejad's electoral victory was backed illegally by well-financed regime elements, including members of the IRGC and the Basij. Mohammad Reza Khatami, Moin's running mate, concluded that they were defeated by what he called "a garrison party." He said, "Until three days before the election, everything was fine; then after a military coup was launched, of which we only learned later, an order was given to a specific military organisation to support a specific candidate, a person whom all the left-wing and the right-wing pre-election pools had shown to be the least favourite among the seven candidates."[45]

The Prowess of the Military

Despite the success of its strategy to find non-Western substitutes for its high-value, high-tech hardware, Iran remains highly interested in access to Western military equipment. The reason for this is twofold. First, in the absence of Iranian access to Japan's military output in terms of the most advanced in Asia, EU and U.S. military hardware remains the best for Iran in terms of technological sophistication. Though the cost is prohibitive in terms of Iran's defense budget today (of little more than $5 billion per year), this hardware's attraction has not waned in Iran. Second, Iran is very conscious that while it has been rekitting its armed forces with Soviet/Russian and Chinese military equipment, all but one of its neighbors (namely, Iraq) have been importing and deploying the best on offer from Europe and the United States. Although in terms of quantity Iran's armed forces may look strong, underneath the surface is the problem of a vast technological gap opening up between

---

[44] Bill Samii, "Observers Fear a Militarization of Politics in Iran," *Radio Free Europe*, November 4, 2005. At http://www.payvand.com/news/05/apr/1072.html.

[45] K. Alamdari, "The power structure of the Islamic Republic of Iran: Transition from populism to clientelism and militarization of the government," *Third World Quarterly*, Vol. 26, No. 8, 2005, p. 1297.

the hardware deployed by Iranian military personnel and that of the neighboring Gulf Cooperation Council countries. It is for this reason, as much as any other, that Iran continues to pursue close and cordial relations with the European Union, in the hope that political and economic ties will eventually lead to security and defense-related ones, too. With an estimated total military budget of around 3 percent of GDP in 2007, Iran is not a serious defense market in regional terms, where the average defense outlay now stands at around 6 percent of GDP—some $70 billion per year.

Thus, the view that Tehran's search for a nonconventional deterrence may also be rooted in its awareness of its relative conventional military inferiority holds very strongly. If it cannot close the gap in the conventional realm, then Iran should try to address the deficit through other means. It is in this context that Iran's arsenal of SSMs becomes a strategic factor. But in the same vein, so, too, is the concern about Iran's active nuclear program and, indeed, its efforts to accelerate the production of such major weapons systems as fighter aircraft, missile systems, and related equipment.

Negotiating with Iran

By Jerrold D. Green

The Challenge and Necessity of Understanding Iran

Americans have been denied sustained access to the Islamic Republic of Iran for almost 30 years. Given the hostility between these two enormously important polities, the implications of this exclusion for the policymaking community have proven to be extremely grave. To appreciate the gravity and significance of this three-decade-long exclusion, it is worth pondering the implications of the fact that virtually no one in today's American policymaking community has ever even been to post-revolution Iran. There are of course exceptions, but no amount of area studies instruction or Persian language study, both important in and of themselves, is a substitute for actually spending time in Iran on the ground. Americans have been denied this to a degree that has proven damaging not only for Washington but also for Tehran. Iran, however, has had and continues to enjoy significant access to the United States.

A considerable number of Iranian elites have studied, lived, or worked in the United States. Despite challenges relating to Middle Easterners securing visas to enter the United States, there is considerable movement back and forth between the United States and Iran because of the large number of Iranian-Americans with family ties to Iran. On the rare occasions that official Iranians meet with their American counterparts, the language of discussion is usually English, showing that in many ways the Iranians know far more about America than do their American counterparts about Iran. Unlike the United States, which lacks a direct foothold in Iran and whose interests there are handled by the Swiss Embassy in Tehran, there is Iranian representation in the United States, in this case via a large Iranian mission to the United Nations in New York. This mission functions as a virtual Iranian embassy in the United States in addition to the Iranian interests section in the Pakistani Embassy in Washington. This permits Iran direct and at times indirect access to the U.S. government, as well as to important interest and other groups throughout the United States.

Furthermore, this mission undoubtedly functions as an important listening post for Iran's representatives, who are able to have a first-hand sense of what is happening in the United States, what American public opinion is concerned with on a real-time basis, and what daily life in America is all about. Iranian officials based in New York can meet with key American business leaders, senators and congressmen, academics, journalists, and others whenever they wish. Despite being restricted to the metropolitan New York area, these Iranian officials have periodically secured permission from the U.S. Department of State to travel throughout the United States. Even high-level Iranian political leaders have direct access to the United States, its government, and its people through visits to the United Nations. President Ahmadinejad's recent visit to Columbia University was only the most recent instance of a high-level Iranian leader having direct access to American opinion leaders and ordinary people. Contrast this to the United States position vis-à-vis Iran, where neither an entry-level analyst at the State Department nor the most senior government leaders can set foot in Iran—be it in Tehran or, in many ways even more important, in Tabriz, Isfahan, Shiraz, Mashhad, and other key areas outside the metropole.

In light of this exclusion from Iran, it is not difficult to understand the challenge that American policymakers have in formulating effective policies toward the Islamic Republic. They do not understand this country, how it operates, its culture, the hopes and aspirations of its people, the organization of its government, its decisionmaking apparatus, where the key levers of power are to be found, how the economy functions, the role of key parastatal *bonyads* in its daily economic life, or, to put it even more simply, what sticks and carrots will induce compliance or promote further resistance and hostility. As evidence of this ignorance, even when it's well intentioned, we only need to look at the facile recommendation of the Iraq Study Group that quite reasonably advocates that the United States seek to engage Iran. This certainly makes great sense, but the devil is in the details, and despite numerous attempts by Washington at different times over the past 30 years to promote engagement or containment, neither approach has been notably effective.

Important responsibility for this failure lies in the ambivalence about and at times outright opposition by the Iranians themselves "to being engaged" by Washington. Yet without greater insight into "how Iran works," American policymakers will continue to be thwarted in their attempts to engage and/or contain Iran—as how does one pressure or beguile a party that one does not know terribly well and understands even less? The staggering costs of ignorance about one's partners and adversaries is being graphically documented almost daily in another setting, Iraq, where we can see what happens when Washington chooses to deal with a context that it little understands. Iran presents a similar challenge, but on an even grander scale. Thus, whatever one's politics or no matter who occupies the White House, the imperative to understand Iran remains and in fact grows steadily in importance. Unfortunately, there is no conclusive evidence that the U.S. government or either political party fully appreciates the burning importance of this task.

Iran Is Unlike Other Countries but Hardly Beyond Understanding

Over the years, there have been numerous attempts to delve deeply into Iranian culture and society to determine what distinguishes Iran from other countries. And although the notion of Iranian exceptionalism is incorrect, this somehow argues that Iran and Iranians are in some way members of a different species. Iran does differ markedly from its neighbors, because all countries have unique attributes. The challenge to any negotiator with Iran is to determine what these attributes are, simply to make the task of negotiating more effective.

In recognition of this important responsibility, the United States Institute for Peace (USIP) launched a long-term cross-cultural negotiations project that in effect attempts to highlight such information in a practical and user-friendly fashion. The effective negotiator will always look for commonalities that the entity he represents shares with the entity with which he is negotiating—so much for exceptionalism, since common attributes can always be found, as well as cultural attributes that distinguish the two but also must be understood. The USIP project has produced individual country studies on a variety of nations, including Russia, Japan, China, Germany, and the like. Reportedly,

John Limbert, a highly qualified former U.S. diplomat who is fluent in Persian and has many years of experience in Iran (primarily before the revolution, although also as a hostage after the upheaval) is preparing a study focused on Iran for USIP. Until this appears, however, we must be content to rely on older sources, many of them quite good, however.

As a rich and ancient culture, Iran has always beguiled outside observers. Yet the complexity and diversity of daily life in Iran have always frustrated those eager to draw simple conclusions based on quick or superficial exposure. This is clearly the case today for Americans who try to understand this hugely complex country based on the speeches of its leaders or the actions of its people seen from thousands of miles away, from "listening posts" in Dubai, or in places where expatriate Iranians may congregate, such as parts of Europe or the United States. Such mechanisms are cumulatively ineffective and indeed potentially dangerous. Certainly the utterances of President Ahmadinejad or some of his equally blunt associates are attention getting. But the question is, particularly in light of the way in which power is distributed in Iran, How significant, representative, and even informative can these flamboyant and provocative utterances be? Fortunately, most Iran watchers are not as uni-dimensional as the President of Columbia University.

Over the years, attempts have been made by observers of Iran to achieve a deeper understanding of what makes this fascinating conundrum of a country "tick." And although much of this scholarship predates the founding of the Islamic Republic in 1979, a new political order does not necessarily signal a complete change in culture, social relations, and the many facets of the wiring diagrams and practices that define a polity. In earlier work done at RAND, I reviewed this literature while trying to discern what sociocultural customs, attributes, and practices defined Iran, both pre- and post-revolution, making it the complex place that it is. Although I cannot review all of this work here, I can say that I relied on pioneering work on Iran by such social scientists as William Beeman, who authored a classic work on *ta'arof*; James Bill, who conducted path-breaking work on social relations in Iran; and Marvin Zonis, who not only wrote on the Iranian political elite, but also tried to discern popular attitudinal factors that resulted from and in turn helped shape and influence Iranian culture and ultimately politics. All three of these scholars spent years living in Iran and are fluent in Persian, and their most pioneering work is still valid because despite a change in political orientation and organization, Pahlavi Iran and the Islamic Republic of Iran are the same country, albeit with important political and other modifications. Although some 65% of the population of Iran is under the age of 25 and knows only the Islamic Republic, I would venture a guess that a comparison with their peers before the revolution would reveal some striking similarities, particularly in the areas that concern us here. And it would be interesting to compare these works to what is currently available in the bookstores by more recent generations of Americans interested in Iran. Although it is certainly not their fault, most of these authors have never been to Iran and do not know the language at all or particularly well. And given these authors' preoccupations with the American policy community for which they write and an American public that now associates everything in the Middle East with September 11—these books are all about U.S. policy and how it can manage relations with Iran better. None of these books is about Iran itself, and here the fault lies primarily in an overly suspicious Iran, which has excluded American scholars and experts and thus left the telling of the "Iran story" to those denied accurate information or interesting things to say because they can't spend any time in the country about which they are writing.

Fortunately, it is not only American scholars who are interested in Iran. Thus, for example, Wilfried Buchta, a German scholar with superb language capabilities, has endeavored with some success to understand how the Iranian system works. Furthermore, it is he more than any other who has shown us how the system has changed during the post-revolution period, since he looks at the Iranian leadership and how elements of it interrelate to one another. His work is extraordinarily detailed and very valuable because he takes as his starting point deep curiosity about Iran as a country and not merely as the object of U.S. policymakers. Iran must be understood internally and on its own terms and not simply from the perspective of foreign policy, both its own and that of the countries with which it interacts politically on the world stage.

Dealing with Iran by Understanding How Iranians Deal with Others

In the earlier RAND work that I conducted on these issues and that I refer to above, I attempted to learn about Iran by consulting non-Americans, since I believe that a particularly effective means to generate such understanding is through talking with those who spend appreciable amounts of time living and working in Iran on a daily basis. Regrettably, virtually no Americans can make this claim. Thus, I conducted extensive interviews with people in a number of countries who deal with Iran not only politically, as do diplomats, but also commercially or in other areas. The logic behind this approach was that in many ways political interactions are frequently the most contentious and fraught with ideologically induced tension. Thus, looking at other types of interactions might help us to better understand the Iranian worldview while avoiding the pitfalls of talking about politics, which frequently raises the very barriers that we hope to understand and hopefully to transcend. Although I cannot fully report on this research here, I would like to share one of the detailed findings I was able to unearth in the form of a written report prepared by someone from the Department of Management of a large Japanese business whose name is familiar to all of us and which has detailed business relationships with and in Iran. Indeed, in many ways I learned more about Iran by talking to Japanese business people than I have in the more traditional post-revolution "American Iran expert community."

In the Japanese written report there are some pedestrian sections and some other, more interesting sections titled: "What is the secret to analyzing conditions in the Middle East" (the answer: "throw away prejudice, pride, and simplistic thinking"); "The intertwining of numerous factors and the frequency of unknown quantities make forecasting difficult," and, most important for the subject of our workshop, "The techniques used in Iran watching." In this very interesting analysis, the author enumerates elements of what he terms "national character." And although national character analysis is out of vogue in the United States, I attribute the use of the term to the author's status as a businessman and not a fashion-conscious American academic with all the trendy intellectual "do's and don'ts" that American academia brings with it.

Among the elements enumerated by this analyst are the following, where he opines that Iranians are (the language here is at times a bit strained as I'm relying on a translation from a Japanese language document):

- Individualistic
- Proud
- Value what's inside
- Hospitality
- Merchant at heart
- Artistic creativity
- Victimization and anti-establishment tendencies

Let me add to this two of the important Zonis findings from his book of 1973, both of which still hold today, in my view:

- Cynicism
- Distrust of authority and political leadership

Finally, I would add the following attributes:

- Feeling of international isolation
- Disappointment at the failures of the Islamic Revolution
  - Internationally (no one substantial has sought to replicate it in their country)
  - Domestically (popular unhappiness about the course of the revolution within Iran)
- Sense of persecution and victimization (historical and current)
- Energetically resist bullying
- Have an idiosyncratic but strongly felt sense of justice
- Prefer consensus to conflict ('ijma in place noted for ijtihad)
- Reluctance to make decisions
- Overlapping decisionmaking centers with inadequate authority

Workshop Discussion Questions

I will end my remarks here, as I would like the above to be the starting point for discussion in our workshop. In addition to discussing the above list and evaluating what is included on it, other questions I would ask all of us to consider and discuss are the following:

- Are the above considerations valid?
- Which are more important and which are less so?
- What are your impressions of and personal experiences in these areas?
- What do Iranian negotiators need to know about their U.S. counterparts?
- Are the issues dividing the two countries so insurmountable that no amount of insight will matter at this juncture?

Understanding Ayatollah Khamenei: The Leader's Thoughts On Israel, the U.S., and the Nuclear Program

By Karim Sadjadpour

There is perhaps no leader in the world more important to current world affairs but less known and understood than Iranian Supreme Leader Ayatollah Ali Khamenei. Neither a dictator nor a democrat—but with elements of both—Khamenei is the single most powerful individual in a highly factionalized, autocratic regime that reaches decision by consensus rather than decree. While Khamenei cannot make major decisions on his own, neither can major decisions in Tehran be made without his consent. This is where his influence has been greatest in the last two decades, blocking and preventing alternative policies rather than initiating ideas and policies of his own.

Khamenei is currently more powerful than he's ever been in his 18-year tenure as leader, for several reasons:

- A highly securitized international and regional atmosphere, which provides a pretext for silencing dissent
- The election of a president who is deferential to him, to his right (making Khamenei appear a moderate), and increasingly unpopular
- The public humiliation of his main rival (Rafsanjani)
- A weak, conservative-dominated parliament, headed by Gholam Ali Haddad-Adel (whose daughter is married to Khamenei's son)
- The rising power of the Revolutionary Guards, whose top leadership is appointed by Khamenei
- The political fatigue of Iran's young population, which has become largely disengaged after the unmet expectation of the reform era.

For these reasons, it is important to take a closer look at Khamenei, his track record as leader, his vision for Iran, and his thoughts on important matters such as U.S.-Iran relations and the nuclear issue.

Khamenei's Iran

Lacking the popular support, charisma, and religious qualifications of his predecessor, Ayatollah Khomeini, Khamenei has often been referred to as a weak and indecisive individual in a powerful post. Domestically his top priority has been to attempt to retain the status quo. Internationally he's been a risk-averse leader—courting neither confrontation nor accommodation with the West—paralyzed by mistrust. His speeches over the last 10 years, however, depict a resolute leader with a remarkably consistent and coherent—though conspiratorial and cynical—worldview.

Four themes dominate Khamenei's political discourse: justice, Islam, independence, and self-sufficiency. From Khamenei's perspective, the 1979 revolution was carried out to achieve these aims, which today the Islamic Republic embodies.[46] These themes are interconnected: Islam embodies justice; independence is not attainable without self-sufficiency; to promote justice and Islam, one must remain independent from foreign powers. From Khamenei's perspective, Iran's enmity toward the United States ("global arrogance") and Israel ("the Zionist entity"), as well as the rationale for Iran's nuclear ambitions, can be explained within this framework.

Khamenei and Israel

Remarkably, the one issue that has featured most prominently in the leader's speeches over the last two decades has virtually no impact on the daily lives of Iranians. From Khamenei's perspective, Israel's usurpation of Muslim lands is the world's ultimate injustice.

On several occasions, Iranian leaders have stated that Tehran will accept any peace agreement that the Palestinians themselves accept. Still, Khamenei has consistently stated that it is armed struggle, not negotiations, that ultimately brings concessions from Israel:

---

[46] "The revolution was staged in the name of Allah and for the sake of justice, independence and freedom. It has since continued its path with the same goals and slogans, and by the grace of God, it will preserve its goals and principles," Leader's Speech to Air Force Servicemen, February 7, 2005.

Over the past seventy years of their occupation of Palestine, the Zionists have not pulled out of even a single square meter of occupied territories as a result of negotiations ... negotiations have never resulted in the liberation of occupied territories and will never do so in the future either." [47]

At the same time, Khamenei has been clear in saying that Iran's goal is not the military destruction of the Jewish state or the Jewish people, but the defeat of Zionism and the dissolution of the Jewish state via "popular referendum":

There is only one solution to the issue of Palestine, the solution which we suggested a few years ago. This solution is to hold a referendum with the participation of all native Palestinians, including Muslims, Jews and Christians, the Palestinians who live both inside and outside the occupied territories. Any government that takes power as a result of this referendum and based on the Palestinian people's vote, whether it is a Muslim, Christian or Jewish government or a coalition government, will be an acceptable government, and it will resolve the issue of Palestine. Without this, the Palestinian issue would not be settled.[48]

For many experienced Iran watchers in both Washington and Tehran, the Islamic Republic's policies toward Israel represent the greatest impediment to U.S.-Iran relations. Not only is Khamenei cognizant of this argument, he is also in agreement with it. Yet it is an exchange he appears unwilling to make:

The ridiculous accusations such as human rights violations or seeking weapons of mass destruction are only empty claims aimed at exerting pressure on the Islamic Republic, and if Iran stops its support of the Lebanese and Palestinian people, the United States will also change its hostile attitude toward the Islamic Republic.... We consider supporting the Palestinian and Lebanese people one of our major Islamic duties. This is why Washington is applying

---

[47]   Leader's Speech to Judiciary Officials, June 28, 2005.

[48]   Leader's Speech to Judiciary Officials, June 28, 2005.

every pressure lever against the Islamic Republic in order to stop this support.[49]

Khamenei and the United States

The second most prominent issue in Khamenei's speeches is opposition and enmity toward the "global arrogance," i.e. the United States. When it comes to the United States, he rarely minces words, especially in response to the hardline rhetoric of the Bush administration:

> Today, the main enemies of Islam are the arrogant powers, and they are led by the United States, which is evil personified and the devil incarnate. This is what we have been saying for the past 24 years.[50]

One thing that is evident both by reading Khamenei's speeches and talking to those personally familiar with him is the fact that he believes that Washington's ambitions are not to change Iran's external behavior but the regime itself. In Khamenei's worldview, the U.S. sees Iran's strategic location and energy resources as too valuable to be controlled by an independent-minded Islamic government. As a result, Washington aspires to put in place a compliant regime in Tehran and revert to the "patron-client" relationship that existed under the Shah:

> The U.S. government has not yet lost its insatiable greed for domination of our country. They are still thinking of restoring their evil domination of Iran, which intensified with the coup on August 19, 1953, and continued until the victory of the Islamic Revolution in 1979. They are still dreaming of the days when the head of state in this country, namely the corrupt and treacherous Mohammad Reza [Pahlavi], made no decisions until he consulted with U.S. officials."[51]

---

[49]   Leader's Speech at International Conference in Support of Intifada, April 24, 2001.

[50]   Leader's Address to Government Officials, May 19, 2003.

[51]   Leader's Address to Education Ministry Officials, July 17, 2002.

In his speeches, the leader pays at least as much attention to addressing the enemy's plots to subvert Islamic Iran as he does to Iran's own national agenda. According to Khamenei's reading of the situation, the U.S. government is intent on seeing the Islamic Republic either go the way of the USSR, gradually decaying and dissolving, or go the way of the 'velvet revolutions' of Eastern Europe, abrupt democratic change spurred by "pro-Western" intellectuals.

> The enemies of our nation and the Islamic Republic, namely the Zionists and the United States, may pin their hopes on two things and try to achieve two goals: first, to convey the wrong idea that our Islamic system is inefficient and unable to fulfill the people's demands and, consequently, weaken the strong relationship that exists between our people and the Islamic system; second, to foment discord and factionalism in our society.[52]

In this context, Khamenei believes Iran cannot afford to compromise in the face of pressure, for compromising as a result of U.S. pressure will only encourage even more pressure:

> The point that should be noted here is that if the officials of a country get daunted by the bullying of the arrogant powers and, as a result, begin to retreat from their own principles and make concessions to those powers, these concessions will never come to an end! First, they will pressure you into recognizing such and such an illegitimate regime, then they will force you not to call your constitution Islamic! They will never stop obtaining concessions from you through pressure and intimidation, and you will be forced to retreat from your values and principles step by step! Indeed, the end to U.S. pressure and intimidation will only come when the Iranian officials, as representatives of the Iranian people, announce that they are ready to compromise Islam and their popular government of Islamic Republic, and that the United States may bring to power in this country whoever it wants![53]

---

[52] Leader's Speech in Mashhad, March 21, 2003.

[53] Leader's Address to Students at Shahid Beheshti University, May 28, 2003.

Khamenei and the Nuclear Issue

It is not really until Iran's nuclear program is revealed to the public that the importance of science and technology becomes prevalent in Khamenei's speeches. He calls overcoming Iran's "scientific retardation" the country's top priority.[54]

For Khamenei, there is a causal relationship between scientific advancement, self-sufficiency, and political independence. His ideal vision is of an Iran that is scientifically and technologically advanced enough to be self-sufficient, self-sufficient enough to be economically independent, and economically independent enough to be politically independent. It is for this reason (and not the proliferation threat), he believes, that the United States is opposed to Iran's scientific, and especially nuclear, advancement:

> They are opposed to the progress and development of the Iranian nation. They do not want an Islamic and independent country to achieve scientific progress and possess advanced technology in the Middle East region, a region which possesses most of the world's oil and which is one of the most sensitive regions in the world.
>
> They are worried about anything that can help the regional nations to achieve independence, self-reliance and self-sufficiency. They want this populous region, which is rich in mineral resources, to be in need of them forever. This is why they are opposed to our possessing modern technology and to our youngsters making progress in scientific areas.
>
> It is hard for the global arrogance to accept that the talented Iranian nation has been able to take great strides in the field of science and technology, especially in the field of nuclear technology. They want Iran's energy to be always dependent on oil, since oil is vulnerable to the policies of world powers. They aim to control other nations with invisible ropes.[55]

---

[54] Leader's Address to University Professors and Elite Academics, October 13, 2005.

[55] Leader's Address to High School Students, March 14, 2005.

When it comes to the nuclear issue, however, it is unclear whether Khamenei purposely misinforms in his speeches in order to maintain appearances of independence and self-sufficiency, or whether he himself is astonishingly uninformed. In addition to consistently invoking the economic benefits of retaining the full fuel cycle (which makes little economic sense), Khamenei has consistently said:

> We are different from those countries that received the technology from the former Soviet Union because they were in the Communist camp. Even China received considerable technological assistance from the former Soviet Union over the first 10 years after its revolution, when the two countries were not at odds yet. However, no country has ever extended any technological assistance to us. We have developed whatever we have ourselves.... We want to produce fuel for our nuclear power plant rather than import it from other countries. What Western countries are saying is that we should not produce nuclear fuel for our Bushehr power plant. They are saying that more nuclear power plants can be built in Iran, provided that we buy the needed nuclear fuel from those countries![56]

Based on Khamenei's rhetoric, there is little indication that Iran would be willing to accede its demand to enrich uranium.

Policy Implications

Over the years, since Khomeini's death, Iran watchers have turned their attention to various individuals and trends in trying to determine the direction in which the country was headed:

- Rafsanjani, Islamic technocrats, and post-war reconstruction (1989–1997)
- Khatami, reformists, the student movement and civil society (1997–2005)
- Ahmadinejad and the Revolutionary Guards (2005–present)

---

[56] Leader's Address to Engineers and Researchers, February 23, 2005.

If there has been one constant throughout these periods and today, it is Khamenei. Both his domestic vision for Iran (more Islamic than democratic) and his foreign policy views (continued enmity toward Israel and the U.S., stopping short of confrontation) have prevailed. He has resisted Rafsanjani and Khatami's desire for accommodation with the U.S., and Ahmadinejad's seeming desire for confrontation. Khamenei speeches in 1995 look remarkably similar to Khamenei speeches given in 2005.

Taking into account Khamenei's unparalleled importance in the Iranian decisionmaking process and his deeply held beliefs and suspicions, any U.S. approach toward Iran should keep several things in mind:

1. Iran will never agree to any arrangement in which it is expected to publicly retreat or admit defeat, or is forced to compromise as a result of pressure alone. Besides the issue of saving face, many in Iran's political elite—chiefly, Ayatollah Khamenei—believe that compromise as a result of pressure projects weakness and will only encourage the United States to exert greater pressure.

2. In order for any diplomatic breakthrough to occur, Washington will need to somehow disabuse Khamenei of the notion that it's bent on the removal of the Islamic Republic government. Indeed, policies should take into account the fact that abrupt revolutionary change is not only highly unlikely, but also undesirable, as currently the only groups armed and mobilized are not liberal democrats but Revolutionary Guardsmen and Bassij militants.

3. In addition to his mistrust of the United States, Khamenei is wary of domestic rivals and will not take any foreign policy decision that may benefit Iran but risk hurting his own political interests. The Clinton administration's unsuccessful attempts to downplay and bypass Khamenei and engage Khatami and the reformists in 2000 are a case in point.

It may not be possible for the U.S. and Iran to reach a diplomatic accommodation as long as Khamenei is leader. After three decades of being immersed in a "death to America" culture, it may be asking too much for Khamenei to reinvent himself at nearly age 70.

The best thing Washington can do is continue the dialogue with Iran about Iraq, simultaneously present it with two distinct paths forward—belligerence will bring isolation while goodwill will beget goodwill—and let it be known that when Tehran is ready to rethink its policies and emerge from isolation, there will be a partner in Washington ready to welcome it.

The Politics of Factionalism in Iran

Draft

By Amin Saikal

Iran's current factional politics is very much a product of Ayatollah Rohullah Khomeini's two-dimensional approach to building and governing Iran as a Shiite Islamic republic: the revolutionary/combative, or "Jihadi," approach and the internationalist/reformist, or "Ijtihadi" approach. Since the mid-1980s, the interplay of these approaches has produced three convoluted and overlapping factional coalitions, which one could label the conservative, the pragmatist, and the reformist. All of them have operated within the Islamic ideological and political framework laid down by Khomeini, and their members have come from similar religious and social backgrounds, cutting across the traditional social-economic layers and class barriers that prevailed in Iranian politics and society prior to the revolution of 1978–79.

Despite the conservatives' control of most of the instrumentalities of the state power since the revolution, Iranian Islamic politics has become highly pluralist, with more than 200 political parties, associations, and organizations now registered in the country. By the same token, the Iranian Islamic regime has grown very much as a Jihadi-Ijtihadi mixture in its content and policy behavior. The stability and longevity of the regime have rested partly on Khomeini's legacy and partly on the favorable environment generated by U.S. policy behavior in the region and beyond. How has this come about? How viable is the regime in the long run in an international order where its independent ideological and policy course of behavior is constantly challenged by the United States and some of its allies?

The origins of Iran's factional coalitions primarily go back to the Society of Assertive Clerics—SAC (Jame'eh Rowhaniyate Mobarez), which formed in 1977 to overthrow the Shah's pro-Western regime in favor of a Shiite Islamic transformation of Iran. SAC's founding members (many of whom were Khomeini's students) included Ali Khamenei, Iran's present Supreme Leader, Seyyed Mohammad Hossein Beheshti, Ali Akbar Hashemi Rafsanjani, and Ayatollah Mahdavi Kani. Although these figures had some differences on the extent to which Islam should underpin politics and economics under the rule of vilayet-e faqih (the Supreme Jurisprudent), they were all initially united in their revolutionary/Jihadi zeal to do away with the Shah's regime.

By the end of 1978, they had all fallen behind Khomeini's call for the Iranian Shiite establishment to abandon its traditional role of overseeing the working of the government in support of taking over the running of the government. Khomeini's call electrified the Shiite clerics, especially the young ones, and established his leadership of the revolution despite his being junior to a number of other Ayatollahs, such as Kazem Shariatmadari and Mahmoud Taliqani.

As the revolution triumphed, the political and social radius of SAC expanded rapidly. It was joined by several other ideologically analogous associations, which had coalesced either before or immediately after the revolution. The three most important of them were the Society of Instructors of the Seminaries (Jame'eh Modarresin Hoze Elmieh—SIS), the Board of Islamic Coalition (Hayate Mo'talefeh Islam—BIC), and the Society of Muslim Engineers (Jame'eh Islami Mohandesin—SME), with the last two representing the traditional merchants of the bazaar, and technocrats. They, like SAC, were fully supportive of Khomeini's approach to transforming Iran into a constitutional theocracy and filled the most important political, administrative, and security positions in the Republic.

Of SAC's founding figures, Beheshti proved to be most politically astute. To unite these associations in a single organization, he urgently moved to set up the Islamic Republican Party (IRP). Although SAC and its associates formed the core of the IRP, they still continued to maintain their individual entities—something that remains the case to the present day. Beheshti was assassinated in 1981, but the IRP rapidly came to act as Khomeini's main organizational backbone, enabling him to pursue a Jihadi approach to Islamizing Iranian politics and society with as much assertiveness (including the use of violence) as required. This is what characterized the first few years of the revolution, with a focus on achieving three main objectives.

The first was to eliminate or weed out those who were closely associated with the Shah's pro-Western dictatorship and to unleash an anti-U.S. rage to humiliate Washington for supporting the Shah's regime. Hence Khomeini's call for the export of the Iranian revolution in order to radicalize Shiite minorities and draw on the political dissatisfaction of some of their Sunni counterparts in the region.

The second was to weaken or marginalize or, in some cases, eliminate those individuals and forces that advocated any thing other than a Shiite Islamic transformation of Iran according to Khomeini's vision. He motivated his supporters to move against such forces as Jabah-i Meli (National Front), the Mujahideen-i Khalq (People's Resistance), and Fedayaeen-i Khalq (People's Sacrificers), as well as those from within his own camp who were deemed undesirable or challenging to Khomeini's Islamic vision. The latter included such figures as senior clerics Ayatollah Kazem Shariatmadari and subsequently Khomeini's designated successor, Ayatollah Hossein Ali Montazeri, who were put under house arrest, and the first elected President of the Islamic Republic, Abol Hassan Bani Sadr, who was forced into exile.

The third was to establish and institutionalize his vision of what constituted an Islamic political order. Hence his adoption of an Islamic constitution and creation of various legal, political, and security structures, as well as a complex system of decisionmaking committees and checks and balances to enforce an Islamic system of governance under the absolute control of the doctrine of Vilayet-e Faqih. He interlinked the operation and functions of the IRP with various paramilitary and security organizations, and used the party as a very potent force to homogenize and monopolize power, enabling his dedicated loyalists to permeate the polity at all levels. As such, he rapidly managed to spawn a very coherent and devoted faction of Jihadi supporters, on whom he could rely to impose what can be best described as a single-frame theocratic order.

However, once the Islamic order was consolidated, the question for Khomeini was how to secure the long-term viability of this order. He seemed to have intended from the beginning that along with his Jihadi efforts he needed to promote an Ijtihadi dimension in order to open the space for a degree of domestic political pluralism and foreign policy flexibility that could help the reconstruction of Iran as an internationally acceptable, strong, modern Islamic state. It was in this context that shortly after the triumph of the revolution, his revolutionary/Jihadi supporters in the IRP underwent a major metamorphosis, giving rise to three informal clusters within the party.

The first was the revolutionary/conservative/Jihadi cluster, which coalesced around such figures as Ali Khamenei and Mohammad Reza Mahdavi Kani. This entity argued for a patriarchal Islamic government, consolidation of the revolution's gains, preservation of a traditional style of life, promotion of self-sufficiency with no dependence on the outside world, and cultural purity.

The second was the reformist/Ijtihadi cluster, which began to evolve from 1987 around leaders like Mehdi Karrubi and Mohammad Khatami. This entity united in its support for a pluralist, democratic Islamic political system. Some of its leading figures, most importantly Khatami, argued for promotion of civil society, relaxation of political and social control, economic openness, cultural renaissance, and more interaction with the outside world. They were inspired by such Iranian thinkers as Ali Shariati and later Abdul Karim Soroush, "who synthesised Islamic moral concepts with modern Enlightenment political philosophy to argue that there was no inherent tension between democracy and Islamic society." But some of its leaders who tended to be more realists than idealists emphasized the importance of maintaining a balance of power in domestic politics.

The third was the centralist/pragmatist cluster, which crystallised around Hashemi Rafsanjani. This entity generally stood between the first and the second and organized itself within two parties—the Executives of Construction Party (Hezbe Kargozaran Sazandegi), which supported the reformists' approach to culture, and the Justice and Development Party (Hezbe E'tedal va Tose'eh), which leaned toward the conservatives on cultural issues. The camp as a whole was inspired by the intellectual work of a number of economic academics, with a belief in economic modernization from above, favoring technical and economic relations with the West, including the United States, but with little evident interest in the democratization of politics. It has flip-flopped on many issues whenever opportune and desirable.

Khomeini seemed quite comfortable with this degree of political pluralism as long as the clusters remained loyal to and operated within his Islamic vision and refrained from public display of their frictions. However, when the IRP faced some factionalist disorder, he pragmatically began to change his stand from the mid-1980s on the legitimacy of a monolithic political organization having a monopoly of power in an Islamic society. He reverted to the traditional Islamist dictum declaring that the existence of any kind of political party in an Islamic entity was inappropriate. By 1987, he formally abolished the IRP and decreed Iran to be a nonpartisan Islamic republic, but without calling for an end to political factionalism as was embodied in the three clusters of his supporters. In parallel with this, he continued to manipulate Iran's external geostrategic settings skillfully, to diversify Iran's foreign relations as a means to minimize the foreign policy consequences of his Jihadi actions, which had isolated Iran from the U.S. and some of its allies.

These developments opened the way for Khomeini's reformist or Ijtihadi supporters to become more active on the political scene to achieve more organizational cohesion and political impact. In March 1998, some of them formed the reformist Assembly of Assertive Clerics—AAC (Majma'a Rowhaniyun Mobarez) under the leadership of Mehdi Karrubi. Initially, some in the AAC leaned toward Rafsanjani's pragmatist centralism, which had helped Rafsanjani win two presidential elections (1989–1997), but not for very long.

Khomeini died in June 1989. The political legacy that he left behind was one of Shiite Jihadi-Ijtihadi politics. This proved instrumental in enabling Khatami from the Ijtihadi side to win two landslide presidential elections in 1997 and 2001, and his reformist supporters to triumph in two parliamentary elections more or less concurrently.

However, the striking feature of the three factional clusters has been that they have all grown to act within the Jihadi-Ijtihadi framework that was promoted by Khomeini as part of what has been deeply embedded in the Shiite theological approach to earthly existence. They have, on the one hand, engaged in power struggles and, on the other, accommodated and overlapped with one another: The conservatives have upheld the ideological purity of Khomeini's legacy, but at the same time proved to be quite pragmatic and reformist whenever needed; the reformists have sought to popularize and pluralize that legacy and make it palatable in the international community, but without losing their sight of their organic linkages with the conservatives; and the pragmatists have straddled between the two whenever opportune. There has been almost a routine fluidity of movement between the clusters, with some of their members changing cluster allegiance quite frequently, and their leaders remaining in consultation meetings from time to time with one another when they have needed to adopt a coordinated position in the face of any serious threat. As such, they have all operated within the limits needed to preserve the Islamic regime.

This is not to claim that the conservatives have not given their reformist counterparts a hard time. They have, largely on the basis of their original domination of the power structure from the time of the Jihadi phase of Khomeini's rule. However, the U.S. refusal to come to terms with the regime and the desire constantly to demonize and threaten it, have also played their parts. Washington's response to the extremism of Iranian conservatives, shaped under the presidency of George W. Bush very much by elements of reborn Christians, neo-conservatives, and ultra-nationalists (all pro-Israel) has helped the cause of the Iranian conservatives at the cost of progressively tightening the space in which the Iranian Ijtihadis can operate. The more the Bush administration and some of its allies, Israel in particular, have threatened Tehran, the more they have forced the Iranian reformists to close rank with their conservative counterparts in the face of a foreign threat. It is not surprising that after the tragic events of September 11, 2001, the conservatives managed to expand their political power further, finally taking back even the legislature and presidency from their reformist counterparts in the 2004 and 2005 elections, respectively. Facing the risk of being accused of "sleeping with the enemy," the reformists have not been able to do much but give ground to their conservative factionalist opponents.

The reformist camp is today very divided. The most liberal amongst them is the Participation Front Party (Jebhe-ye Mosharekat), led institutionally by Mohammad Reza Khatami, the brother of former President Khatami, and intellectually by Saeed Hajjarian and his associates. The second most influential and disciplined party is the Organization of Strivers of the Islamic Revolution (Sazmane Mojahedine Enghelab Eslami). The third non-clerical group is the Solidarity Party (Hezbe Hambastegi), whose major leading figure is Ibrahim Asgharzadeh, one of the leaders in the 1979 hostage-taking fiasco, atlhough he now asserts that such action is detrimental to world peace and Iran's foreign relations. Indeed, many leading reformists are now critical of the radical conservatism that they displayed in the first few years of the revolution. The least modern group amongst the reformists remains the AAC, which is led by Mohammad Mousavi Khoeiniha and is mainly affiliated with Ayatollah Hossein Ali Montazeri.

It is this degree of inter-cluster operability that has changed the face of Iranian politics since the early years of the revolution. It has made Iranian politics more pluralist than is the case in many neighboring Arab countries, with greater scope for increased discussion and criticism and more political and social mobility. The conservatives have maintained their dominance, but from Ali Khamanei and President Mahmoud Ahmadinejad down, they have come to embrace a number of policy formulations and practices of the pragmatists and reformists as their own. They have done so in the knowledge that they either have to change in line with the requirements of a changing Iran and world, or else risk the future of the Islamic regime. In a sense, the need for politics of regime preservation has led them to acquiesce to some pluralist changes, as a result of which Iran cannot be regarded as strictly a theocratic state any longer.

Whatever President Mahmoud Ahmadinejad's Jihadi rhetoric, he has ultimately had little choice but to carry many of his Ijtihadi opponents with him. He has essentially risen from the ranks of those followers of Khomeini that the latter called the musta'zafeen ("the have nots," or dispossessed) as against mustakbareen ("the haves," or oppressors), and it is this category that overwhelmingly voted for him and what he claims to represent. This has led him to engage in a kind of Islamic politics which he thinks would endear him not only to the Iranian musta'zafeen, but also to their counterparts in the Muslim world, most importantly in its Arab domain. Hence his provocative anti-American and anti-Israeli pronouncements, as well as his uncompromising position on Iran's nuclear program, which he claims to be for peaceful purposes, but which Washington and some of its allies suspect to be for nuclear weapons. He is criticized for his failures on the economic front by elements from all factional clusters, including his own, and in the sphere of foreign policy by many reformists. But ultimately he has the support of leaders from across the factional spectrum when it comes to such matters as the nuclear issue and U.S. and Israeli threats. Despite the widespread perception outside Iran, he maintains good relations with the Supreme Leader, and despite dislike of him by many in the major urban centers, he remains popular with rural Iran, where he has invested much time and energy. On all issues important, he essentially echoes the Supreme Leader, who is the ultimate power holder and has proved to be both Jihadi and Ijtihadi in his supervision of Iran's domestic and foreign policy.

If today the Islamic leadership and, for that matter, Iran are in a position of greater regional influence than ever before, it has a great deal to do with American policy failures rather than anything substantial that Iran has done in the region. The U.S.'s disastrous handling of the Iraqi, Afghan, Palestinian, and Lebanese situations, as well as the so-called war on terror, has created massive strategic vulnerabilities for the U.S., but favorable strategic opportunities for the Iranian regime and Shiite Islam to become more assertive than ever before.

What has resulted regionally is an Iran-led Shiite strategic entity stretching from western Afghanistan, which is closely linked to Iran, across to Lebanon, where Hizballah is a major political and military player. Iran's links with many powerful elements of the Iraqi Shiite majority and its strategic alliance with Syria form the central pieces of the entity. The profound shift that has occurred in the sectarian and strategic balance has confronted the U.S. and its allies with critical challenges and dilemmas. Neither the U.S. nor its Arab and non-Arab allies want Tehran to be the main beneficiary of their policy failures.

Whatever the future direction of U.S. policy behavior, the Iranian regime is set to play a critical role in shaping regional politics. Its Jihadi-Ijtihadi politics has come to interact dramatically with American policy failures in Iraq in particular and in the region in general. Whether Ahmadinejad or someone else is at the helm, no Iranian leader can now afford to go too far beyond a Jihadi-Ijtihadi approach. It is within this approach that even the current leadership is capable of cutting a deal with the U.S., based on politics of mutual need and vulnerability, given Iran's dire economic situation and need for outside, especially American, help, and America's need for Iranian assistance to bail it out of its regional difficulties. However, this can only come about if first Washington accepts the Iranian political order as legitimate and stops threatening it as a pariah in world politics. A window of dialogue has already opened in this respect with the U.S. and Iranian ambassadors to Iraq having held two direct meetings this year. The challenge for both sides is now how to build on these meetings toward a rapprochement independent of what can be dictated by the interests of third parties—such as Israel and some Arab states—in the region. If they fail to meet this challenge, the alternative is military confrontation, from which neither can emerge victorious in view of what they are capable of doing against one another.

Economic Decisionmaking in Iran

Draft

By Koichiro Tanaka

1. Introduction

The Iranian market, with a population of roughly 70 million, one of the largest in the region, is viewed as offering a bright opportunity for entrepreneurs, industrialists, financiers, and trade houses from the industrialized countries, including Japan, and from developing economies. Yet, undeniable statistical figures, as well as the general reputation of the actual business conducted by Japanese enterprises with and in Iran, represent the gloomier side of the picture: a market that is extremely difficult to penetrate and establish oneself in.

By providing an overview of Iranian economic policy and decisionmaking, this paper will try to address the practical difficulties that are associated with commerce, trade, and investment in Iran, which is just another mirror image of the political entanglement of a country that is rich in resources, talents, and opportunities but has not been successful in tapping them adequately.

2. The General Structure

While the desire for control over the economy by the government remains relatively high, today's Iran follows two sets of policy frameworks that govern its economic policy: (a) the 20-year long-term perspectives drawn by the Supreme Leadership, and (b) the five-year development plans (FYDPs) that are prepared and implemented by the government in power. The long-term perspective is a virtual guideline that is associated with macroeconomic targets set forth for the long run, whereas the successive FYDPs have been designed in conformity with the long-term perspective, to adjust and rectify the country's structural problems, which have become hindrances to Iran's economic development and a healthy economic policy.

Ever since the first FYDP was introduced in 1990 with an objective to promote reconstruction, development, and liberalization of the economy, two successive governments of Rafsanjani and Khatami have spared no effort to tackle inflation, unemployment, inefficiency, and incompetency through structural reform of the country's war ravaged economy. The Iranian economy badly needed to reduce its dependency on oil export revenues, curtail government overspending, and adjust monetary policy in order to control inflation.

Following an absence of over one decade, foreign direct investment (FDI) was sought seriously by the government, exhibited by sizzling debates in the Majles, as a booster to invigorate the economy. Foreign loans and financing for development projects were another issue, for which the Rafsanjani presidency circumvented the constitutional red line by introducing the buyback scheme that later led to application to the oil and gas sector. The Law on Attraction and Promotion of Foreign Investment (LAPFI), a fossil legislation introduced in 1955, was the only tool to entice foreign investors who sought, in their eyes, better and more promising opportunities in places like Dubai. The comparative disadvantage had pushed the Khatami government to prepare and introduce the Foreign Investment Promotion and Protection Act (FIPPA) in 2000.

A relaxation of trade policies followed by an attempt to unify multiple foreign exchange rates were subsequently introduced as other key elements of economic reform. Following some ups and downs during the 1990s, the exchange rate was finally unified during Khatami's second presidency in order to be instrumental in promoting a more liberalized economy.

When it comes to anatomizing the mechanism of major economic policymaking, the primary authorities involved would be: the ministers with responsible portfolios, the Majles as a whole and individually its relevant commissions, the Supreme Economic Council chaired by the president, the Guardian Council with vetting powers to reject legislation by the Majles, and the Expediency Council as an advisory board to the Supreme Leader. Other entities enjoy some say in policies or sometimes unevenly large influence. Such bodies range from the local councils that are closer to the grassroots, to the government-controlled media at the top. Apart from these entities, High Council for Investment chaired by the Minister of Economy and Finance, High Council of Free Trade Zones working directly beneath the president (in case of FTZs), the Supervisory Board for the Attraction and Protection of Foreign Investment, along with the Organization for Investment, Economic and Technical Assistance of Iran (OIETAI), a subsidiary of the Ministry of Economy and Finance, are the authorities that are responsible for the attraction of FDI.

Other relevant institutions to be noted here would be the Ministries of the Interior, Labor and Social Affairs, Customs Agency, Iranian Privatization Organization (POI), and the Central Bank of Iran (CBI).

The semi-official or even the non-official bodies, like the local Basij squadron that is composed of the devotees to the Islamic Revolution and the Imposed War and the Chamber of Commerce, Industry and Mines, which partially represent the private sector, get themselves involved as pressure groups with abilities to exert influence on key decisionmaking bodies. In between stand the official Bonyads, like the Bonyad-e Mostazafan, and the recently attention-getting IRGC subsidiaries, which both have high stakes in the semi-state economy, but also enjoy strong personal relationships with key political players.

The judicial system could and would, although it has limited leverage to influence economic policies, become an extremely important player once the policies are implemented, with its relevant legislation and regulations inured.

In short, since it would be no exaggeration to state that roughly a dozen governmental bodies are involved and mobilized in the economic policy decisionmaking process, the challenges that any government may face in its effort to coordinate the individual interests among them would be serious.

3. Barriers, Obstacles, and Interferences

Some ideas work out much better than they sound or, on the contrary, some things look far better on paper than in reality. In the case of the Iranian economy, although in recent years the external indicators have displayed continued signs of improvement owing to the higher oil prices, it often tends to be the latter.

In the past, many external analyses have been made public, questioning the resolution among the political leadership to reform, the efficiency of the bureaucratic system, and the capacities of individual officials. Although stalled by the strong U.S. and Israeli opposition to Iran's application to join the WTO, the required structural reform for the ascendancy is far from over. Regarding the tax system reform, the VAT has constantly been on the aggressive agenda since the early 1990s, and is again targeted to be introduced from the next fiscal year, 1387 (2008–09).

Complexity caused by the existence of overlapping and competing governmental and semi-governmental entities and agencies since the early days of the Islamic Revolution has hampered the implementation of certain policies. But, in reality, these phenomena were just another display of the ongoing political competition among various power centers, or factions, and commercial entities with strong ties to the leaders of the regime and the clergy.

At times, decisions taken by the same government have contradicted each other and in the end, have undermined its designed effect on the economy. The actual usage of the Oil Stabilization Fund, or the OSF, first created under the Fourth FYDP, displays clear signs of inconsistency with its designed noble objective. It has constantly become a hotbed of political debate and power struggle among various factions, usually ending up in sponsoring additional government spending.

Lack of coordination within the government, associated with its rather common flip-flop in interpretation and implementation of the policy, has not impressed foreign capitals. FDI, thus, has not materialized in the way it was supposed to. Lack of FDI is even evident in the oil and gas sector, and concern was voiced by Petroleum Minister Vaziri-Hamaneh, who subsequently lost his portfolio as a minister.

Nor has the privatization target been met. According to an IMF Report of March 2007, since the late 1980s, complicated regulatory and legal structures and weak political support traditionally prevented an effective implementation of the program. While promoting privatization, favors and preferential treatment were still provided to state-owned entities, which only would dissuade the capital market from participating in IPOs. Conflict between the stipulation of the Constitution's Article 44 and the government's policy had virtually put the program under hibernation for years until a recent comprehensive directive was issued by the Supreme Leader, Ayatollah Khamenei, to resolve the matter. It is now expected that the program would get back on its track while firmly excluding the upstream oil sector, crucial infrastructure, and some of the state-owned banks from privatization.

Discrepancies between the government and the Majles over the same issue have cut off certain policies at the knees, as evidenced in the normalization of the fuel and utility prices. Toward the final year of the Khatami presidency, the Majles had suspended the program, and since then, for more than three years, the additional cost for importing oil products, inter alia gasoline, had to be allocated, solely depending on the OSF for its resource, before the rationing system was introduced in summer 2007. Suggested reform of the buyback agreement scheme has fallen into this trap, as well.

Currently, under the Ahmadinejad presidency, the focus of the Iranian priorities has shifted from structural reform toward reducing social and regional disparities. Distortion of the economy, comprising extensive administrative controls on prices and interest rates, aggravated by heavy government spending, especially by this president, is worsening every year through the provision of subsidies, both obvious and hidden, on various goods and services. Ahmadinejad's strong commitment to draw down interest rates of banks in order to tame inflation to single digits, which has put the independence and the function of the Bank-e Markazi (CBI) under serious questioning, is again a policy that would eventually be like shooting himself in the foot.

In the Islamic Republic, too much political control or, in another phrase, interference, both at the policy decisionmaking level and the implementation of policies, is possibly spoiling the economy! For the politicians, the economy remains their "tool" to gain greater power.

4. Practical Examples

There are particular examples that shed light on the difficulties that the Japanese have faced in doing business with Iran. Iran's external relationship, especially with the U.S., has definitely raised the stakes, while the internal difficulties will illustrate the basic challenges Iran's economic policies need to address and have been addressing.

For the Japanese businesses, as well as other Western companies, taxation has become one of the chief irritants for the managers and the employees to deal with. Since the late 1990s, the National Iranian Tax Administration (NITA) has introduced a taxation system according to a uniform standard for levying corporate taxes against foreign representative offices that are operating under the sole purpose of maintaining their representative(s) in Iran while not conducting any commercial, industrial, or financial activity. Because of the mounting pressure to enforce the regulation, one Japanese oil company that enjoyed a long-standing relationship with Iran, but also had defied the international embargo against Iranian oil during the Mossadegh era, was forced to choose indefinite closure of its historical representative office in Tehran.

In contrast to this case, Japanese commercial banks that are obligated by the CBI to position personnel as liaisons in Tehran if the main offices wish to handle Iranian transaction L/Cs are not subject to the uniform standard; whereas, since the late 1990s, a personal income tax, based on the supposed nominal income of the person according to his or her title and nationality, is levied heavily against the foreign staff of the offices, even though the assumption would be way above the salary that the said staff is earning.

These moves are considered to be a backlash of the government's incapability to raise tax revenues as projected in the national budget each year, making non-Iranian entities and personnel easy targets since they would all be vulnerable to entry, residential, and exit visa problems if they do not comply with the instructions and orders from the authorities.

The extra burden created by the government's inconsistent and incoherent policy hampers efforts to conduct even daily business. Even when a directive addressing certain issues in favor of the foreign partners is issued by head offices of ministries as well as the CBI, it is often observed that the message is not properly communicated to and implemented by the subordinate offices, raising serious questions over the line of communication and the limits of the bureaucratic system.

There are other relevant reports that are worth noting. Sudden, and often confusing, operational changes introduced through issuance of bylaws or change of personnel at the managerial level have pressed the businesses to maintain close contact with relevant government officials. The absence of adequate legal coverage and support that govern business activities, glacial moves to adjust impeding regulations, barriers in remitting profits despite the stipulation of FIPPA, and a bureaucracy affected by factionalism and political contention—these are all part of other impediments that the Japanese have to contend with.

It is certain that any entity, regardless of being Iranian or non-Iranian, would have to equally abide by the law. Yet factional rivalries should not become excuses for arbitrary enforcement of some of the regulations that would not only discredit the trust against the Iranian government, but also obstruct the creation of the fair and free environment that is a prerequisite to economic development.

5. Conclusions: Learning Lessons

As displayed above, both the complexity in decisionmaking and the existence of various competing power centers in Iran contribute to portraying the Islamic Republic as an extremely confusing system, giving priority to political expediency over economics. It is thus often difficult to ascertain where the real policy goals lie, even for those who are working for the system. As far as the economic policy is concerned, the prevailing style is unlikely to work in Iran's favor, since many potential investors, partners, customers, and clients could and would be dissuaded to work in or with an environment that could inflict unpredictable damage. The current imposition of both UNSC and U.S. unilateral sanctions may have negatively impacted the market, but still, the lagging progress in attracting FDI since the early 1990s to date is strongly indicative of some other reasons.

Negotiating with Iranian business counterparts is said to be stimulating, since they always see room in negotiation, as opposed to the business-like yet dry negotiating style of "take it or leave it" that prevails in some of their Arab neighbors. But be aware that even when the final accord has been reached, your Iranian counterpart may approach you seeking a last-minute renegotiation over the settled conditions in their favor. This may become frustrating and embarrassing to you, especially when you are in front of your company executives who have flown thousands of miles to ink the agreement. They might just want to make a good impression on their bosses, but the bottom line is that they are obsessed about being cheated and exploited by others.

For sure, the Iranians are tough negotiators, as they have proved themselves throughout history, and in the region, but also in the current nuclear crisis.

Iran in the Arab Sphere: Debating Legitimacy, Sovereignty, and Regional Order

By Fred Wehrey

Since the 1978–79 Islamic Revolution, the question of Iranian power and its role in the region has been a central, if not always dominant, feature of Arab official and public discourse. Whether conventional military threat, steadfast champion of the Palestinian cause, usurper of Arab territory, or beleaguered victim of Western double standards on the nuclear issue, Iran has been subjected to divergent Arab interpretations—many of which reveal more about insecurities and fissures in the Arab system than they reveal truths about the Islamic Republic.[57]

This paper will offer a brief survey of these diverse perceptions, covering fluctuations in Arab public opinion since the fall of Saddam, inter-Arab debates over Iran's nuclear ambitions, and the sectarian dimension of Arab-Iranian relations. It posits that Arab deliberations on the Iranian threat make up a sort of code for expressing deep-seated problems of political legitimacy, sovereignty, relations with the West, and regional hierarchy. Shrill warnings from Arab leaders of a "Shiite crescent" are most illustrative of this; Iran's "new" assertiveness is more a challenge to the stagnant political order than any sectarian threat to Sunnis per se.

Understanding these dynamics, this paper concludes, is critical for U.S. policy toward the Islamic Republic. Increasingly, U.S. policymakers have turned to Arab regimes as interlocutors, interpreters, and allies against Iran, but they need to understand the complex set of local interests and agendas that inform these roles. Moreover, the U.S. cannot separate the challenge of Iran from the Arab sphere, particularly the Gulf; Iran both influences and is influenced by the perceptions of its Arab neighbors.

---

[57] For a sample overview of Arab threat perceptions, see 'Abd al-Rahman al-Rashid, "Li Hathahi al-Asbab, Nukhasha Iran" (For These Reasons, We Fear Iran) (in Arabic), *Al Sharq Al Awsat*, April 18, 2006.

"More Arab Than the Arabs": Iran in the Public Realm

Writing in July 2007, a popular columnist for *Al Sharq Al Awsat* urged his readers to "examine all the big Arab portfolios—Lebanon, Palestine, and Iraq. They are being stolen from Arab hands ... and turned over to Iranian hands gradually."[58] Iran has long pursued a policy of speaking over the heads of Arab regimes directly to their populations, presenting itself as "more Arab than the Arabs," traditionally on Palestine, but increasingly in Iraq.[59] To justify their involvement in Iraqi affairs, for example, Iranian leaders have highlighted Iran's role in inspiring the anti-British 1920 revolt in Iraq—a seminal event in the Iraqi nationalist narrative that has resonated throughout the region.[60]

Yet Iran's hyper-activism on pan-Arab issues is not necessarily proof of its influence, but rather just the opposite—an effort to over-compensate for its fundamental isolation from the rest of region. Despite its claims to universalism, it remains the odd man out. By its own admission, it has largely failed in its attempt to refashion the Arab world in its image, reflected most visibly by the fact that its principal Arab Shiite "clients" in the Gulf (the Islamic Front for the Liberation of Bahrain, the Organization for the Islamic Revolution on the Arabian Peninsula, and the Supreme Council for the Islamic Revolution in Iraq) have all distanced themselves from their erstwhile patron, through name changes or a more substantial reorientation of goals.[61]

---

[58] Mshari al-Dhaydi, "Warning to the Religious Establishment" (in Arabic), *Al Sharq Al Awsat*, July 19, 2007 (available as of October 17, 2007, at http://www.asharqalawsat.com/leader.asp?section=3&issue=10430&article=424347).

[59] For background on this strategy, see Trita Parsi, "Israel and the Origins of Iran's Arab Option: Dissection of a Strategy Misunderstood," *Middle East Journal*, Vol. 60, No. 3, Summer 2006.

[60] This claim predates the Islamic Revolution, as highlighted by Jasim Abdulghani, *Iraq and Iran*, London, 1984, p. 21; quoted in Fred Halliday, *Nation and Religion in the Middle East*, Boulder, Colo.: Lynne Rienner, 1984, p. 109.

[61] The Islamic Front for the Liberation of Bahrain became the Islamic Action Society, the Organization for the Islamic Revolution on the Arabian Peninsula became the Reform Movement, and the Supreme Council for the Islamic Revolution in Iraq recently became the Supreme Islamic Iraqi Council.

Nonetheless, Iran's belief, whether warranted or not, that it can draw support from Arab publics has impelled Tehran toward brinksmanship and bravado in its foreign policy. This is nowhere as evident as in the brazen posturing of Ahmadinejad, who received widespread applause in the Arab public realm for his populist, grassroots appeal and his outspoken critique of the status quo—all of which contrasts sharply with many of the Arab world's cautious and frequently septuagenarian rulers. An illustrative example of this dynamic was Ahmadinejad's speech denying the Holocaust in the presence of King Abdullah at a 2005 summit in Mecca. To the al-Saud, who have portrayed themselves as the region's preeminent patrons of the Palestinians, the Iranian president's remarks were a brazen act of one-upsmanship, which left them mortified and unable to respond.[62]

Yet Iran's appeal can quickly fade when regional events are "read" through a sectarian or Arab-Persian prism. In some cases these events are beyond Iran's control; in others they result from its own strategic missteps. Most notably, the collateral acclaim that Iran garnered after Hizballah's 2006 war with Israel quickly dissipated in the wake of the December 2006 Saddam execution, which was widely viewed as an Iranian and U.S.-engineered attempt to diminish Arab identity.[63] On Iran's Arabic satellite TV, *Al Alam*, a commentator appeared perplexed by this reaction, questioning why the "Arab media are intentionally using the execution of Saddam Husayn to foment sectarian conflict" and concluding that "those who are mourning Saddam ... are worried about their shaky thrones."[64] By 2007, available polling and media surveys revealed a noticeable drop in Arab public support for Iran—stemming principally from worsening sectarian violence in Iraq. Zogby's 2007 polling of 3,400 Arab respondents in Egypt, Saudi

[62] Renaud Girard, "The Calculated Provocations of the Islamist Iranian President" (in French), *Le Figaro*, Paris, December 19, 2005.

[63] Open Source Center Analysis, January 10: "Saddam Execution Stokes Arab Anti-Iran, Anti-Shia Sentiment," GMF20070111222001, *Middle East—OSC Analysis* in English, January 10, 2007.

[64] Open Source Center, "Iran's Al-Alam TV Discusses Arab Reaction to Saddam's Execution," IAP20070102950094, Tehran, *Al-Alam* (in Arabic), 1330 GMT, January 2, 2007.

Arabia, Jordan, the UAE, and Lebanon showed that a majority believed Iran's role in Iraq was unhelpful, although there was broad consensus that U.S. actions were similarly detrimental.[65]

To combat anti-Iranian themes in the official Arab media, Iran employs a well-developed architecture of transnational outlets to reach Arab audiences. Although bolstered by recent technical advances, this strategy is not new; the importance of "psychological warfare" has long been a fixation of Iran's revolutionary leadership. For example, in a 2006 Arabic monograph on the subject, *Dur Wasa'il al-A'lam fi al-Sira' al-Siyasi wa al-Thaqafi* (The Role of Media in Political and Cultural Conflict), Supreme Leader Ayatollah Ali Khamenei praised the effects of radio, TV, and other media in cultivating Islamic ideals after the revolution, mobilizing Arab support for Hizballah, and deflecting Western misrepresentations of the Islamic Republic.[66]

In general, however, Iran's media aspirations in the Arab sphere have fallen short. Its major transnational Arab media outlet, *Al Alam*, has lagged behind its pan-Arab competitors, *Al Arabiya* and *Al Jazeera* in terms of credibility and popularity, according to available media surveys.[67] Even among Iran's Shiite co-religionists in Saudi Arabia's

---

[65] When asked about their greatest regional worry, respondents were split, with U.S. permanence in the region, the fragmentation of Iraq, and the spillover of the Iraq war generally outweighing the direct threat of Iranian hegemony. James Zogby, "Four Years Later: Arab Opinion Troubled By Consequences of Iraq War" (available as of August 27, 2008 at http://www.aaiusa.org/page/-/Polls/2007_poll_four_years_later_arab_opinion.pdf).

[66] Ayatollah Ali Khamenei (edited by Shaykh 'Ali Dhahir), *Dur Wasa'il al-A'lam fi al-Sira' al-Siyasi wa al-Thaqafi* (The Role of Media in Political and Cultural Conflict), Beirut: Dar al-Hadi for Printing, Publishing and Distribution, 2006, pp. 39–59.

[67] Open Source Center, "BBC Monitoring: Iran's Al Alam TV Plays Role in Arab Media Scene," GMP20070115950064, Caversham, UK: *BBC Monitoring* in English, January 15, 2007; "BBC Monitoring: Iran Media Guide," IAP20070327950024, Caversham, UK: *BBC Monitoring* in English, March 27, 2007. However, in the months following the fall of Saddam, a State Department INR poll noted that *"al-Alam* was the most trusted and watched television station in Iraq, behind the Iraq Media Network (IMN) and the religious Najaf channel." This probably stemmed from *Al Alam's* availability as the only non-Iraqi terrestrial station whose signal can be received without a satellite dish. By 2004, however, an Intermedia Survey reported that 78 percent of Iraqi viewers had access to satellite dishes and that *Al Alam's* total audience reach was put at 15 percent compared to over 60 percent for the most popular channels, *Al Arabiya* and *Al Jazeera*. Moreover, the station received only single

Eastern Province, the channel is viewed as heavy handed and too ideological, according to RAND interviews in early 2007.[68]

One issue where Iran has enjoyed continuing support from Arab publics is regarding its right for nuclear energy. As noted earlier, this endorsement has less to do with Iran per se and is more accurately an oblique attack on Western interference in the region and double standards, particularly concerning Israel.[69] It also raises the broader question of inter-Arab debates on Iran's nuclear program, to which we now turn.

The Nuclear Impasse: Renegotiating Arab Hierarchy

The Iranian nuclear impasse has amplified Arab insecurities about an impending shake-up in the regional order and opened new fissures—between regimes and their publics, but also among Arab states. On the implications of a nuclear Iran, there are significant differences in Arab perception between states of the northern and southern Gulf, between Saudi Arabia and the rest of the GCC, and between Iran's "near abroad" and countries farther west, particularly Egypt.

Many states, especially smaller GCC countries, appear to fear the consequences of a U.S. strike more than the implications of a nuclear-armed Iran. This has resulted in a strong accommodating impulse by some smaller states, represented most explicitly by Oman. "Why should we be more afraid of a nuclear Iran than a nuclear Pakistan?" a senior Omani military commander stated during a RAND

---

figures for reliability and importance as a source of information. See Open Source Center, "BBC Monitoring: Iran Media Guide," IAP20070327950024, Caversham, UK: *BBC Monitoring* in English, March 27, 2007; and "Iraq Television Viewership Poll," U.S. Department of State, Office of Intelligence and Research, October 16, 2003.

68   RAND discussions with Shiite religious leaders and activists in Qatif, Dammam, and al-Ahsa, Eastern Province, Saudi Arabia, March 15–21, 2007. According to one respondent, a noted Shiite intellectual, even Hizballah's television station *Al Manar* was not popular among Saudi Shiites, because it consistently adopted a tone that was critical of Iraqi Shiite parties, such as SCIRI/SIIC, toward which the Saudi Shiites showed a strong affinity. It was not until the 2006 Lebanon war that *Al Manar*'s resonance increased, largely because of its compelling battlefield footage.

69   Open Source Center, "BBC Monitoring Analysis: Arab Dilemma Over Iran's Nuclear Program," FEA20070627206546, OSC Feature, *BBC Monitoring*, June 27, 2007.

discussion in early 2006. Elsewhere in the Gulf, the UAE is concerned that a nuclear Iran will grow more belligerent in its diplomacy on the disputed Abu Musa and Tunb Islands, although even within the UAE there are splits. A Foreign Ministry official in Abu Dhabi pointed to Dubai's more accommodating posture toward Iran, arguing that this presented an opening for Tehran to exploit. In the northern Gulf, Kuwait is most concerned about the environmental consequences resulting from an accident at an Iranian reactor.[70]

The reaction of Saudi Arabia to a nuclear Iran will likely be the pivot around which the rest of the region turns. Smaller states perceive that Riyadh is exploiting the Iranian threat to dominant Gulf affairs, positioning itself as Washington's anti-Iranian proxy. The centrality of Saudi Arabia in the recent U.S. arms sale proposal would appear to confirm this suspicion, while Ahmadinejad's offers to collude with Saudi Arabia on "filling the regional power vacuum" in Iraq after a U.S. withdrawal further unsettles old paradigms of regional order. Several officials in the smaller Gulf states argued that Washington should "watch its friends first," meaning Saudi Arabia, with one former diplomat arguing that Saudi Salafi ideology was the region's "real nuclear bomb."[71]

Aside from Saudi-GCC frictions, there are divisions between the GCC and the Levant. Specifically, Gulf states in Iran's immediate environs believe that old pan-Arab norms on the Israeli nuclear threat, embraced more strongly by Egypt and the Levant, are increasingly

---

[70] These insights are derived from my interviews in Oman, the UAE, Kuwait, Bahrain, and Saudi Arabia during February 2006, November 2006, and March 2007. For more on Gulf and regional perceptions of the nuclear impasse, see Dalia Dassa Kaye and Frederic M. Wehrey, "A Nuclear Iran: The Reactions of Neighbours," *Survival*, Vol. 49, No. 2, Summer 2007, pp. 111–128; Karim Sadjadpour, "The Nuclear Players," *Journal of International Affairs*, Vol. 60, No. 2, Spring/Summer 2007, pp.125–134; Richard L. Russell, "Peering Over the Horizon: Arab Threat Perception and Security Responses to a Nuclear-Ready Iran," Non-Proliferation Policy Education Center, February 5, 2005, available at http://www.n-epc.org; Judith S. Yaphe and Charles D. Lutes, "Reassessing the Implications of a Nuclear-Armed Iran, McNair Paper 69, Washington D.C.: National Defense University, 2005; Simon Henderson, "The Elephant in the Gulf: The Arab States and Iran's Nuclear Program," *Policy Watch 1065*, Washington Institute for Near East Policy, December 21, 2005.

[71] Author interviews with senior Gulf diplomatic officials, February 2006.

detrimental to their interests.[72] Accordingly, these regimes have contended that Egypt is tacitly supporting an Iranian bomb as a countervailing deterrent against its more proximate enemy, Israel, or to give itself a pretext for withdrawing from the NPT and pursue its own capability. Turning this logic around, a prominent Kuwait think-tank scholar has proposed a tacit GCC endorsement of Israel's bomb as a deterrent against Iran.

From Egypt's perspective, the Saudi reaction to Iran is most worrisome; Cairo will not sit idly if its rival claimant for Arab leadership pursues a nuclear capability, and appears similarly alarmed at any moves toward Saudi-Iranian cooperation. Commenting on the Abdullah-Ahmadinejad summit in March 2007, Egyptian analysts questioned whether the tentative Iranian-Saudi coordination on Lebanon, Palestine, and Iraq was "pulling the political rug from underneath Cairo's feet" and lamented Egypt's deepening retreat from Arab affairs.[73]

All of this suggests that, from the Arab perspective, the Iranian nuclear problem is not so much about mitigating the threat of a direct nuclear attack, but rather about resolving long-standing tensions in the Arab system that this impasse has exposed. In attempting to build Arab consensus, U.S. policymakers should be mindful of how these parochial concerns can complicate or even sabotage their efforts against Iran.

"A Country Acting Like a Sect": Iran and Anti-Shiism

One concern expressed by Arab states, especially in the Gulf, is that a nuclear-armed Iran would inspire Arab Shiite populations toward greater activism and even militancy. The prospect of a U.S. withdrawal from Iraq and recent Iranian offers to fill the "vacuum" have only intensified these fears. A recent editorial in *Al Sharq Al Awsat* lambasted Iran for behaving like a "sect" and for embracing the same colonialist logic

---

72 Emile El-Hokayem and Matteo Legrenzi, *The Arab Gulf States in the Shadow of the Iranian Nuclear Challenge*, working paper, The Henry L. Stimson Center, May 26, 2006.

73 Open Source Center, "Cairo Political Analysts View Implications of Iranian-Saudi Rapprochement," GMP20070309007003, Cairo: *Al-Misri Al-Yawm* in Arabic, March 9, 2007, p. 4 (Report by Khalifa Gaballah: "Experts: Iran mapping the future of the region together with Saudi Arabia in the absence of an Egyptian role").

of vacuum-filling that informed America's Middle East intervention following Britain's "east of Suez" withdrawal in 1971.[74]

Here again, such rumblings are more accurately seen as windows into deeper problems of political illegitimacy and governance. Nowhere is this more apparent than in Bahrain, where the regime has traditionally used the specter of Iranian omnipotence to portray any moves toward reform and democratization as "sectarian" or "Iranian backed." And as noted earlier, the real threat posed by Iranian or Iranian-backed Shiite actors, such as the Lebanese Hizballah, lies in their populist, nonsectarian challenge to the status quo political order— witness analogies drawn by Egyptian oppositionists to "Nasser 1956/ Nasrallah 2006" during the Second Lebanon War, which coincided with the fiftieth anniversary of the nationalization of the Suez Canal.[75] Arabic Posters bearing the visages of Hugo Chavez, Nasser, Nasrallah, and Ahmadinejad are a more visual example.[76]

To mitigate this, some Arab regimes have played up the sectarian dimension of the Iranian challenge, to curry popular support for what is essentially a balance-of-power strategy against Iran. As noted by F. Gregory Gause III, anti-Shiism is a way to "sell" an anti-Iranian policy and dampen public enthusiasm for Iran's defiant nuclear posture.[77] Thus, we see in Saudi Arabia the recirculation of old anti-Shiite and anti-Iranian fatawa, many of which originate in the Saudi-Iranian ideological "cold war" of the 1980s. One key example is the renewed popularity of an anti-Khomeinist book written shortly after the revolution, purportedly by a prominent cleric at the Islamic University of

---

[74] Bilal al-Hasan, "Ahmadinejad's Grave Mistake: The Theory of Vacuum Filling" (in Arabic), *Al Sharq Al Awsat*, September 2, 2007.

[75] Morten Valbjørn and André Bank, "Signs of a New Arab Cold War: The 2006 Lebanon War and the Sunni-Shi'i Divide," *Middle East Report*, Spring 2007, p. 7.

[76] For more on this dynamic, see Graham Fuller, "The Hizballah-Iran Connection: Model for Sunni Resistance," *The Washington Quarterly*, Vol. 30, No. 1, Winter 2006, pp. 139–150.

[77] F. Gregory Gause III, "Saudi Arabia: Iraq, Iran, the Regional Power Balance and the Sectarian Question," *Strategic Insights*, February 2007.

Medina; the tract was quoted extensively by Abu Musab al-Zarqawi in a four-hour diatribe recorded shortly before his death in June 2006.[78]

The most immediate casualties of this trend are Arab Shiite populations, particularly on the Arabian Peninsula. Increasingly, Bahraini, Saudi and, to a lesser extent, Kuwaiti Shiites have been portrayed by Salafi hard-liners and some regime officials as either disloyal "fifth columns" for Iran or as agents of fitna (sectarian discord).[79] A notable example is President Hosni Mubarak's televised declaration that the Arab Shiites' "loyalty is always to Iran" and "not to their countries."[80] In Saudi Arabia, a senior Sunni establishment cleric accused the Kingdom's leading Shiite figure, Hassan al-Saffar, of promoting takfir (excommunication) of Sunnis.[81] Such accusations, however, are largely unjustified; Gulf Shiites generally regard Iran with spiritual and emotional affinity, rather than as a political model for emulation. Many appear unwilling to jeopardize hard-won political gains made in the

---

[78] The book is by Muhammad 'Abdallah al-Gharib, believed by many analysts to be a pseudonym for Muhammad Surur Zayn al-Abidin, an influential Syrian-born cleric at the Islamic University of Medina. *Wa Ja'a Dur al-Majus* (And Then Came the Turn of the Magi), 1988 (available as of October 19, 2007, at http://www.tawhed.ws/a?i=402). The transcript of the Zarqawi audio recording, *Hal Ataka Hadith al-Rawafidh?* (Has Word of the Rejectionists (Shiites) Reached You?) is available as of October 15, 2007, at http://www.tawhed.ws/r?i=4048.

[79] Frederic M. Wehrey, "Saudi Arabia: Shi'a Pessimistic on Reform, But Seek Reconciliation," *Arab Reform Bulletin*, June 2007 (available as of October 19, 2007 at http://www.carnegieendowment.org/publications/index.cfm?fa=view&id=19217#wehrey). Also, Toby Craig Jones, "Saudi Arabia's Not So New Anti-Shiism," *Middle East Report*, No. 242, Spring 2007, pp. 29–32.

[80] Mubarak's statement was carried on *Al Arabiya* TV, April 9, 2006. Also, Anon., "Tactless Mubarak Provokes Reassertion of National Loyalties by Gulf Arab Shias," *Gulf States Newsletter*, Vol. 30, Issue 779, April 14, 2006. In Egypt, this tactic is not new; recall that the Islamic Revolution animated Muslim Brotherhood activists, prompting Sadat to emphasize its narrow sectarian motives. Rudee Mathee, "The Egyptian Opposition on the Iranian Revolution," in Juan R. I. Cole and Nikki R. Keddie (eds.), *Shi'ism and Social Protest*, New Haven: Yale University Press, 1986, pp. 247–274.

[81] Shaykh Hassan al-Saffar, *La wa Lan Nuqbil Aya' Marja'n Takfiri'an wa Arfad Tadkhal aya' Marja' fi al-Shu'un al-Siyasi al-Dakhili li-Biladna* (We Do Not And Will Not Welcome Any *Marja'* [Spiritual Reference] That Promotes *Takfir* [Excommunication] And We Oppose The Interference of Any *Marja'* in the Internal Political Affairs of Our Country) *Al-Risala*, February 16, 2007.

1990s to serve as Tehran's retaliatory proxies. In some cases, Shiite intellectuals on the Peninsula, particularly in Saudi Arabia, have been vocal critics of the legitimacy of the Iranian political system, with a resonance that extends well beyond the Gulf.[82]

Yet despite their protestations of loyalty, Gulf Shiites perceive a palpable stall in domestic reform initiatives, which many attribute to Washington's recent focus on building Arab support against Iran, rather than democracy promotion.[83] Ironically, this loss of momentum, combined with the hardening of Sunni opinion, could actually reinforce the Shiites' sectarian identity, radicalizing their increasingly youthful populations, and creating new openings for Iranian influence that might not have otherwise existed.

Conclusion

This paper has surveyed how the question of Iranian power has intensified long-standing fissures between Arab regimes and their publics, divisions over inter-Arab hierarchy, and sectarian tensions related to deeper problems of governance and the absence of pluralism. Understanding these multidimensional effects is of critical importance for U.S. policymakers who seek Arab support against Iran. Every Arab state that elects to align itself with the U.S.—whether as a stalwart military ally or diplomatic interlocutor—has a deeper set of domestic and regional calculations in mind that may diverge completely from Washington's. Thus, U.S. policies toward Iran will inevitably reverberate in the Arab sphere, perhaps in unintended ways and to the potential detriment of other U.S. interests.

---

[82] Examples include Shaykh Tawfiq al-Sayf, *Nathiriyat al-Sulta fi al-Fiqh al-Shi'i* (Theories of Political Power in Shiite Jurisprudence), Beirut: Center for Arabic Culture, 2002; and Shaykh Hassan al-Saffar, *Al-Madhhab wa al-Watan* (Sect and Homeland), Beirut: Arab Foundation for Studies and Publishing, 2006.

[83] In a February 2006 interview with the author, a prominent Salafi reformer and legal expert in Riyadh warned that tensions with Iran would result in a curtailment of social and political reforms; this was subsequently echoed in follow-up interviews with other reformists, activists, and intellectuals in Jeddah, Riyadh, and the Eastern Province in March 2007.

Iran's Oil Sector: Questions, Puzzles, Explanations

Draft

By Charles Wolf, Jr.

I. Iran and the "Resource Curse"

Iran's economy is a special example of what in the backwaters of economic literature is referred to as "the resource curse" or, alternatively, "the Dutch disease."[84] The terms were intended to describe certain economic pathologies displaying the following symptoms: (1) development of a scarce resource that commands large economic rents **for** the endowed economy and **from** the rest of the world; (2) a resulting surfeit of internal liquidity and capital inflows that boost the exchange rate, attract capital and labor to the resource-favored sector, and inflate domestic demand; (3) in turn, price inflation is triggered, productive factors are siphoned away from the non-favored sectors, and thereby more balanced, durable, multisector economic development is impeded.

Neglected in the literature dealing with these pathologies, and probably of equal if not greater importance than the symptoms themselves, is a propensity that the flood of economic rents induces in the country's policymakers to indulge in sometimes wasteful, perverse, and corrupting economic policies.

With respect to the symptoms associated with the "resource curse," Iran is at once a classic example as well as a special case with some distinctive facets and paradoxes of its own. As such, its economy presents a range of questions and puzzles to which this paper seeks to provide preliminary answers.

---

[84] See Amber Moreen, "Overcoming the 'Resource Curse,'" PRGS Dissertation, RGSD-215, Santa Monica, Calif.: RAND Corporation, 2007. Also see W. M. Corden, "Booming Sector and Dutch Disease Economics: Survey and Consolidation," Oxford Economic Papers 36, Vol. 33, 1984. *Dutch Disease* was originally intended to refer to the perverse economic consequences of discovery and development of rich natural gas deposits off the Netherlands coast in 1970. One should be cautious about pushing the premise of "resource curse" too far. There are also notable counter-examples of resource benefactions: for example, Norway, Britain, and North Sea oil and gas deposits.

Toward this end, we have analyzed a large set of data about Iran's economy, with particular focus on the oil sector. The raw data are not included in this draft. What follows below are the eight principal questions we have asked of the data, and the preliminary answers arrived at thus far.[85] The apparently slight differences in the wording of several of the questions is designed to highlight specific aspects of the "resource curse."

We are well aware that there are many puzzling questions about the Iranian economy that can't be answered by available data; for example, questions relating to the scale and content of military spending, the distribution of income and wealth currently and over the nearly three decades since the revolution, the extent and reality of "privatization" of state-owned enterprises, and so on. Section II is an initial attempt to see how far the data can take us in answering several relevant and interesting questions. For readers who are interested in a "bottom-line" trope, rather than the detailed answers, Section III distills these along with a few concluding observations.

II. Questions, Puzzles, and Preliminary Answers

(1) How sensitive is Iran's GDP and its growth to variations in Iran's oil production **volume** (measured in tons or barrels)?

That the Iranian economy is heavily dependent on oil is well known. The aim of this question as well as several of the following ones is to calibrate more precisely the extent and magnitude of the dependence. The unsurprising, short-form answer to the first question is: "highly sensitive." Nearly 93 percent of the variation in Iran's GDP over the period from 1976 to 2006 is explained by variations in the volume of oil production and passage of time. Expressed quantitatively, an increase of 1 percent in oil production is associated with an increase

---

[85] The exploratory analysis on which the answers are based consists of simple linear and log linear regressions of selected dependent variables on specified independent variables. For example, in question (1), the selected dependent variable is GDP, and the specified independent variable is the volume of oil production. Subsequent equations test the respective influence of oil production value and oil export value, as alternative explanatory variables. Unless otherwise indicated, all of the results are statistically significant at a 5 percent level.

of 0.22 percent in GDP. At the same time, this result also indicates that three-quarters of increases in GDP are attributable to other production than that of oil.

(2) How sensitive is Iran's GDP to variations in the **value** (measured in U.S. dollars) of Iran's oil production?

Iran's GDP is equally sensitive to changes in the value (reflecting price as well as production) of Iran's oil output. Slightly more than 93 percent of the variation in GDP is explained by variations in the value of oil production and time; if production value increases by 1 percent, Iran's GDP would be expected to increase by 0.18 percent.

(3) How sensitive is GDP to variations in the value of Iran's oil **exports**?

The answer to question 3 is that GDP is still more sensitive to variations in export value than to variations in production and production value. While not surprising, the quantities involved are striking: 98 percent of the variation in Iran's GDP is explained by variations in the value of its oil exports and the passage of time in the three decades covered by our data. Each increase of 1 percent in Iran's oil export value would be expected to increase GDP by a nearly equal amount: 0.92 percent!

(4) How closely correlated are Iran's oil production, world oil prices, and the value of Iran's oil exports?

As suggested by the preceding questions and answers, the several influences on Iran's GDP are correlated with one another, although differentially so. For example, the simple correlations between the value of oil export value and the value of oil production, between production value and global oil prices, and between oil export value and global oil prices are all very high (greater than 0.90). In contrast, the simple correlation between the volume of oil production and global oil prices is quite low (0.37)—presumably a reflection of the influence of technical and other physical obstacles to expanded production, and perhaps to a lesser extent of OPEC quotas and global oil prices.

(5) How sensitive is Iran's domestic consumption of oil, gasoline, and other refined products to GDP, to oil exports, to world oil prices, and to domestic oil prices?

This question is intended to explore the determinants of Iran's domestic consumption of oil and refined products. Our analysis indicates that for each increase of 1 percent in Iran's GDP, domestic consumption of oil, gas, and other refined products can be expected to increase by 0.67 percent.

Oil exports also affect domestic consumption of oil and refined products, but to a lesser degree: an increase of 1 percent in the value of oil exports results in an expected increase in domestic consumption of oil and refined products of 0.37 percent.

One special aspect of Iran's version of the "Dutch disease" is a perverse paradox that links oil exports to GDP (see question 3, above), and GDP to domestic consumption of oil and oil products (question 5): Oil exports tend to increase GDP, and increased GDP tends to increase domestic consumption of oil and refined products, which, in turn, tends to lower oil exports! The second link in this chain—increased domestic consumption of oil and ORP—is, presumably, reinforced by a policy of maintaining a huge (i.e., 90 percent) subsidy on domestic energy consumption. Stated another way, the elasticity of domestic oil (or energy) demand with respect to GDP (or GNI) tends to be high because oil and energy prices are so low.

(6) How sensitive are Iran's oil exports to world oil prices?

The answer is "not very sensitive"; indeed, the effect of oil prices on Iran's oil exports is slightly negative! While suggestive, this result is not statistically significant. More specifically, an increase of $1 dollar per barrel in the price of oil leads to a decrease of 11,000 barrels per day (or 0.5 percent) in the volume of Iranian oil exports—another paradox in the Iranian version of the Dutch disease.

(7) What is the relation between Iran's oil exports and (a) Iran's money supply (M2), and (b) inflation (CPI)?

In this instance, Iran's economy appears to function more or less in accord with standard economic precepts. With respect to subquestion 7(a): on average, an increase of 1 percent in the volume of oil exports leads to an increase of 0.68 in money supply; variations in oil exports explain nearly 60 percent of variations in M2 over the period covered by our data; with respect to subquestion 7(b): on average, an increase of 1 percent in the money supply is associated with an increase of 1.6 percent in the consumer price index, and variations in the money supply explain 87 percent of variations in Iran's double-digit inflation.

(8) How are oil export revenues divided among the government budget, ministerial budgets, Revolutionary Guards, national oil corporation, other state enterprises, partly privatized state enterprises, bonyads, and other entities?

In 2006, Iran's oil exports of about 2.5 million barrels a day (from production of about 4.0 million bbl/day) generated foreign exchange earnings of $50 billion; earnings in 2007 will be over $60 billion. "Where the money goes" in Iran, no less than in other countries, is a significant indicator of where power and influence lie and of the country's national priorities.

Although available data don't allow precision in answering this question, we are engaged in a preliminary attempt to describe the money trail, and plan to present and discuss this at the Rome conference.

III. Summary and Conclusions

That the Iranian economy is heavily driven by oil—production, value, and exports—is, of course, well known. The magnitude of this relationship is less well known: 98 percent of the variation in Iran's GDP over the past three decades is explained by variations in the value of its exports. Allowing for the passage of time, for each increase of 1 percent in the value of Iran's oil export earnings, GDP would be expected to increase by a nearly equal amount: 0.92 percent!

While many aspects of the relation between oil and Iran's macroeconomy represent a classic example of the so-called "resource curse," a.k.a. "Dutch disease," the Iranian case also has certain aspects that are unique to it. The perversely circular relation between oil exports, GDP, domestic consumption, and oil exports is an example. Oil exports increase GDP, and increased GDP increases domestic consumption of oil, gasoline, and other refined products, which, in turn, tends to decrease oil exports. This perverse sequence is aggravated by a long-standing, politically sensitive policy of heavily subsidizing domestic energy consumption. Thus, the elasticity of energy consumption with respect to income changes tends to be higher than if full (opportunity) cost pricing of energy prevailed. A further perverse consequence is that, because Iran's domestic refining capacity is limited, increases in domestic consumption of refined products in turn generate increased imports, rather than increased domestic production and employment.

Iran's oil exports are relatively insensitive to changes in world oil prices. Although the regressions we've run on this relationship show a slightly negative association between price changes and exports, the coefficients are not statistically significant. What the data suggest, however, is that when oil prices rise, Iran's oil exports are as likely to fall as they are to rise.

In trying to fathom the interplay among interest groups, politics, national security, religion, economic policy, and social policy, the general precept "to follow the money" seems relevant in Iran no less than in other countries. A preliminary attempt to describe this pattern is conveyed by a few charts and schematic diagrams that we are still working on and plan to present at the conference.

Biographies of Workshop Participants

Shahram Chubin

Shahram Chubin is Director of Studies at the Geneva Centre for Security Policy, Switzerland. He has been a Director of Regional Security Studies at the International Institute for Strategic Studies (IISS) and has taught at various universities, including the Graduate School of International Studies in Geneva and the Fletcher School of Law and Diplomacy. A specialist notably in the security problems of the Middle East region, he has been a consultant inter alia to the U.S. Department of Defense, the Hudson Institute, and the United Nations. He has been a resident fellow at the Wilson Center, the Carnegie Endowment, and the Hudson Institute.

He received his B.A. from Oberlin College, Ohio, and his Ph.D. from Columbia University, New York City.

Chubin has published widely in journals such as *Foreign Affairs, Foreign Policy, International Security, Washington Quarterly, Survival, Daedalus,* The Middle East Journal, *The World Today,* and *The Adelphi Papers.* His recent publications include a chapter on the domestic politics of Iran's nuclear ambitions in the latest *Strategic Asia* volume (Washington, D.C., National Bureau of Asian Research, 2007); *Iran's Nuclear Ambitions* (Carnegie Endowment, 2006); "Whither Iran? Reform, Domestic Policy and National Security," IISS Adelphi Paper 342 (London: Oxford University Press for IISS, 2002); and, with

Robert Litwak, "Debating Iran's Nuclear Aspirations," *The Washington Quarterly*, Autumn, 2003.

Other publications include: (as co-author), *Iran's Security Policy in the Post-Revolutionary Era,* Santa Monica, Calif.: RAND Corporation, 2001 (available at http://www.rand.org/pubs/monograph_reports/MR1320/); "Iran's Strategic Predicament," *The Middle East Journal,* Vol. 54, No. 1, Winter 2000, 10–24; (with Jerrold D. Green), "Engaging Iran," *Survival,* Vol. 40, No. 3, Autumn 1998, 153–167; "A Pan-Islamic Movement: Unity or Fragmentation?" Chapter 3 in A. Jerichpow and J. Baek Somonsen (eds.), *Islam in a Changing World,* Curzon Press, 1997; (with Charles Tripp), "Iran-Saudi Arabia Relations and Regional Order," Adelphi Paper 304, London: IISS, 1996; "Does Iran Want Nuclear Weapons?" *Survival,* Vol. 37, No. 1, Spring 1995, 86–104; *Iran's National Security Policies: Motivations, Capabilities, Impact,* Carnegie/Brookings 1994; (with Charles Tripp), "Domestic Politics and Territorial Disputes in the Persian Gulf and Arabian Peninsula," *Survival,* Winter 1993–94; "The South and the New World Order," *Washington Quarterly,* Vol. 16, No. 4, 1993; (ed.), *Germany and the Middle East: Problems and Prospect,* London: Pinter; New York: St. Martins, 1992; "Postwar Gulf Security," *Survival,* April/May 1991; (with Charles Tripp), *Iran and Iraq at War,* London: Tauris; Boulder, Col.: Westview, 1988; (with Sepehr Zabih), *Iran Foreign Relations,* University of California, 1974.

He has also contributed chapters to numerous books, including Geoffrey Kemp and Janice Stein (eds.), *Powderkeg in the Middle East: The Struggle for Gulf Security,* Maryland: Rowman & Littlefield (for the AAAS), 1995; Patrick Clawson, *Iran's Strategic Intentions,* McNair Papers 29, Washington D.C.: National Defense University, 1994; Alex Danchev and Dan Keohane (eds.), *International Perspectives on the Gulf Conflict 1990–91,* London: Macmillan, 1994; Robert Litwak and Mitchell Reiss (eds.), *Nuclear Proliferation After the Cold War,* Wilson Center/John Hopkins, 1994; Rosemary Hollis (ed.), *The Soviets, Their Successors and the Middle East,* London: St. Martins (for RUSI), 1993.

In addition, Chubin has published articles in *The Times* (London), *The International Herald Tribune, Le Temps, The Observer* (London), *New Society* (London), *Die Zeit* (Hamburg), *Weltwoche* (Zürich), *Temp*

Strategique, Le Temps (Geneva), and *Vanguardia* (Barcelona). He has also been a frequent contributor to the *BBC World Service* (radio and TV).

James F. Dobbins

James F. Dobbins directs RAND Corporation's International Security and Defense Policy Center. He has held U.S. Department of State and White House posts, including Assistant Secretary of State for Europe, Special Assistant to the President for the Western Hemisphere, Special Adviser to the President and Secretary of State for the Balkans, and Ambassador to the European Community. He handled a variety of crisis-management assignments as the Clinton administration's special envoy for Somalia, Haiti, Bosnia, and Kosovo, and as the Bush administration's first special envoy for Afghanistan.

Dobbins was the lead author on the 2005 two-volume set titled *RAND History of Nation-Building* (Vol. 1, *America's Role in Nation-Building: From Germany to Iraq*; Vol. 2, *The UN's Role in Nation-Building: From the Congo to Iraq*; both of which are available at http://www.rand.org/pubs/monographs/MG304.1/) and the 2007 *Beginner's Guide to Nation Building*, available at http://www.rand. org/pubs/monographs/MG557/.

In the wake of September 11, 2001, Dobbins was designated the Bush administration's representative to the Afghan opposition. He helped organize and then represented the United States at the Bonn Conference, during which a new Afghan government was formed. On December 16, 2001, he raised the flag over the newly reopened U.S. Embassy.

Dobbins graduated from the Georgetown School of Foreign Service and served three years in the U.S. Navy.

Anoush Ehteshami

Anoush Ehteshami is a professor of international relations and head of the School of Government and International Affairs at Durham University. He is also a Fellow of the World Economic Forum. He was Vice President of the British Society for Middle Eastern Studies (BRISMES) from 2000 to 2003.

His current research revolves around five over-arching themes: (1) the Asian balance of power in the post–cold war era; (2) the "Asianisation" of the international system; (3) foreign and security policies of Middle East states since the end of the cold war; (4) the impact of globalization on the Middle East; (5) good governance, democratization efforts in the Middle East.

His many book-length publications include *Globalization and Geopolitics in the Middle East: Old Games, New Rules*, New York: Routledge, 2007; (with Mahjoob Zweiri), *Iran and the Rise of its Neoconservatives,* London: I.B. Tauris, 2007; (as co-editor), *The Middle East's Relations with Asia and Russia,* London: Routledge Curzon, 2004; (as co-editor), *The Foreign Policies of Middle East States,* Boulder, Col.: Lynne Rienner, 2002; (as co-author), *Iran's Security Policy in the Post-Revolutionary Era,* Santa Monica, Calif.: RAND Corporation, 2001; (as co-editor), *Iran and Eurasia,* Reading: Ithaca Press, 2000; *The Changing Balance of Power in Asia*, Abu Dhabi: ECSSR, 1998; (with Ray Hinnebusch), *Syria and Iran: Middle Powers in a Penetrated Regional System*, London: Routledge, 1997; (as co-editor) *Islamic Fundamentalism*, Boulder, Col.: Westview Press, 1996; *After Khomeini: The Iranian Second Republic,* London: Routledge, 1995; (ed.) *From the Gulf to Central Asia: Players in the News Great Game*, Exeter: University of Exeter Press, 1994; (as co-editor), *Iran and the International Community,* London: Routledge, 1991; *Nuclearisation of the Middle East*, New York, NY: Brassey's Defence Publishers, 1989.

Jerrold D. Green

Jerrold D. Green is Senior Advisor for Middle East/South Asia and Director of the Middle East Development Council at the RAND Corporation in Santa Monica, California. In these roles, he is responsible for expanding the work conducted by RAND throughout the Middle East and South Asia. Prior to his current employment at RAND, he served as a partner and Executive Vice President for International Operations at Best Associates in Dallas, Texas, where he was also Executive Vice President for Academic Affairs of Whitney International University System. Before joining Best Associates, he served as Director of International Programs and Development and Director of the Center for Middle East Public Policy at RAND. He has also served as a Visiting Professor in the School of International Relations at the University of Southern California and in the Department of Political Science at UCLA.

Green has a B.A. (*summa cum laude*) from the University of Massachusetts/Boston, and an M.A. and Ph.D. in political science from the University of Chicago, where he specialized in the politics of the Middle East. Green's career began at the University of Michigan, where he was a faculty member in the Department of Political Science and the Center for Near Eastern and North African Studies. He subsequently joined the University of Arizona, where he became a Professor of political science and sociology and Director of the Center for Middle Eastern Studies.

Green uses Arabic, French, and Persian in his work and has lived and worked in Egypt, where he was a Fulbright Fellow, and Iran. He has also spent considerable time in virtually all of the other Middle East countries. His work has been supported by such organizations as the Social Science Research Council, the American Research Center in Egypt, and the Smith Richardson Foundation. He travels frequently to the Middle East and has lectured extensively on six continents. Green has been a Visiting Fellow at the Chinese Academy of Social Science's West Asian Studies Center in Beijing, a visiting lecturer at the Havana-based Center for African and Middle East Studies (CEAMO), a Fellow at the Australian Defense College, and a presenter at international conferences sponsored by the Iranian Institute of International Affairs in Tehran. At Best Associates, he engaged in business activities in numerous countries: Argentina, Brazil, China, Colombia, Costa Rica, Liberia, Mexico, Panama, Philippines, and others. Green is a member of the Council on Foreign Relations and the Middle East Studies Association, and has served on the Advisory Committee of the Asia Society of Southern California. He is the Deputy Director of the Los Angeles County Sheriff's Department Office of Foreign Relations, as well a Specialist Reserve Police Officer with the Los Angeles Police Department, where he advises the Anti-Terrorism Division on Middle East issues. He also serves as a member of the Advisory Boards of Cappello Capital Corporation Investment Bankers in Los Angeles, The Conektas Group in Dubai, Columbia University's Middle East Institute in New York, and the International Advisory Board of the Whitney International University System in Dallas. He is a technical advisor to Activision Publishing in Santa Monica, California, the world's largest producer of video games.

Green has written widely on Middle East themes, focusing on American Middle East policy, the role of religion in the region, inter-Arab relations, Iranian politics, and the Arab-Israeli conflict. His work has appeared in such publications as *World Politics*, *Journal of Comparative Politics*, *Ethics and International Affairs Journal*, *Survival*, *Middle East Insight*, *Politique Etrangere*, *The World Today*, *The RAND Review*, *The Harvard Journal of World Affairs*, and *The Iranian Journal of International Relations*.

Karim Sadjadpour

Karim Sadjadpour is an associate at the Carnegie Endowment for International Peace. He joined Carnegie after four years as the chief Iran analyst at the International Crisis Group based in Tehran and Washington, D.C. A leading researcher on Iran, Sadjadpour has conducted dozens of interviews with senior Iranian officials and hundreds of interviews with (among others) Iranian intellectuals, clerics, dissidents, paramilitaries, businessmen, students, activists, and youth.

He is a regular contributor to *BBC World* TV and radio, *CNN*, *National Public Radio*, and *PBS* and has written for many newspapers, including the *Washington Post, New York Times, International Herald Tribune,* and *New Republic.* He is frequently called upon to brief U.S. and EU officials about Middle Eastern affairs. As a result, he has testified before the Senate Foreign Relations Committee; given lectures at Harvard, Princeton, and Stanford universities; and has spoken before the Council on Foreign Relations and Asia Society.

Sadjadpour was named a "Young Global Leader" by the World Economic Forum in Davos, Switzerland, and has received numerous academic awards, including a Fulbright scholarship. He has lived in Latin America, Europe, and the Middle East. He has a B.A. from the University of Michigan and an M.A. from Johns Hopkins School of Advanced International Studies. He speaks English, Farsi, Italian, and Spanish.

Sadjadpour's recent commentary, articles, and testimony include "Britain-Iran Standoff," *PBS's Newshour with Jim Lehrer,* March 29, 2007 (available at http://www.carnegieendowment.org/publications/index.cfm?fa=view&id=19082&prog=zgp&proj=zdrl,zme); "Was Iran's Seizure of Britons Response to U.N.?" *NPR* interview, March 28, 2007 (available at http://www.carnegieendowment.org/publications/index.cfm?fa=view&id=19081&prog=zgp&proj=zdrl,zme); "American Scholar Released from Iranian Jail" *NPR's* All Things Considered, August 21, 2007 (available at http://www.carnegieendowment.org/publications/index.cfm?fa=view&id=19529&prog=zgp&proj=zme); "The Wrong Way to Contain Iran," *International Herald Tribune,* August 3, 2007 (available at http://www.carnegieendowment.org/publications/index.cfm?fa=view&id=19473&prog=zgp&proj=zme); "Revolutionary Guards Have Financial Interest in Keeping Iran Isolated," Council on Foreign Relations interview, May 29, 2007 (available at http://www.carnegieendowment.org/publications/index.cfm?fa=view&id=19464&prog=zgp&proj=zdrl,zme).

Amin Saikal

Amin Saikal is a political science professor and Director of the Centre for Arab and Islamic Studies (The Middle East and Central Asia) at the Australian National University. He is a specialist in the politics, history, political economy, and international relations of the Middle East and Central Asia.

Saikal has been a Visiting Fellow at Princeton University, Cambridge University, and the Institute of Development Studies (University of Sussex), as well as a Rockefeller Foundation Fellow in International Relations (1983–1988). In April 2006, he was appointed Member of the Order of Australia (AM) for service to the international community and to education through the development of the Centre for Arab & Islamic Studies and as an author and adviser. He is also a member of many national and international academic organizations.

He has written numerous works on the Middle East, Central Asia, and Russia, including *Modern Afghanistan: A History of Struggle and Survival*, I.B. Tauris, 2004; *Islam and the West: Conflict or Cooperation?* London: Palgrave Macmillan, 2003; (as co-editor), *Lebanon Beyond 2000*, Canberra: Centre for Middle Eastern and Central Asian Studies, Australian National University, 1997; *The Rise and Fall of the Shah*, Princeton University Press, 1980; (as co-author), *Regime Change in Afghanistan: Foreign Intervention and the Politics of Legitimacy*, Westview Press, 1991; (as co-editor), *Islamic Perspectives on the New Millennium*, Singapore: Institute of Southeast Asian Studies, 2004; (as co-editor), *Democratization in the Middle East: Experiences, Struggles, Challenges*, New York: United Nations University Press, 2003; (as co-editor), *The Soviet Withdrawal from Afghanistan*, Cambridge University Press, 1989; (as co-editor), *Russia in Search of Its Future*, Cambridge University Press, 1995.

Saikal has also published numerous articles in international journals, as well as many feature articles in major international newspapers, including the *International Herald Tribune*. He is also a frequent commentator on radio and television.

Koichiro Tanaka

Koichiro Tanaka is Director of the Japanese Institute of Middle Eastern Economics (JIME) Center and Manager of the Iran Group at the Institute of Energy Economics, Japan (IEEJ), Tokyo. He started his career in 1989 at the Embassy of Japan in Tehran as a political attaché; he then joined JIME in 1992 as a senior researcher to study events related to Iran. In 1998, he left JIME to serve as Political Affairs Officer of the United Nations Special Mission to Afghanistan (UNSMA), which was headed by Ambassador Lakhdar Brahimi and his successor, Ambassador Francesc Vendrell. In October 2001, after completing his mission, Tanaka joined the International Development Center of Japan; in June 2004, he returned to JIME. The merger of JIME and the IEEJ in April 2005 led to his current responsibilities.

Tanaka received a B.A. in Persian linguistics from the Faculty of Foreign Language, Tokyo University of Foreign Studies, and an M.A. in Persian linguistics from the graduate school of the same university in 1988. He has contributed to several books and to numerous study programs and presentations at international conferences in the fields of international relations and regional development in the Middle East, preventive diplomacy, and peacemaking/-building, as well as energy security. He has appeared on the podium of the 10th and 11th Institute for International Energy Studies (IIES) Oil and Gas Forum in Tehran, Iran.

Along with his research activities, Tanaka contributed to the International Observation for the Election/Selection of the Emergency Loya Jirga in May to June 2002 and the two EU missions for the observation of presidential and parliamentary elections in Afghanistan in 2004 and 2005, respectively.

Frederic Wehrey

Frederic Wehrey is an International Policy Analyst at RAND Corporation, currently researching Gulf security, Saudi-Iranian relations, and future U.S. policy in the Middle East. Prior to joining RAND in July 2005, he served as an active-duty U.S. Air Force officer for 10 years, with analytic and operational assignments throughout the Middle East. In 2003, he deployed to Baghdad with the Iraq Survey Group, earning the Bronze Star. His most recent military assignment was on the Joint Staff at the Pentagon, where he served as an Iran analyst, producing daily assessments for the Chairman of the Joint Chiefs of Staff and the Secretary of Defense.

Wehrey holds a B.A. in Middle Eastern History, with honors, from Occidental College in Los Angeles, and an M.A. in Near Eastern Studies from Princeton University. His articles on Shiite activism, regional perceptions of Iran, and the Lebanese Hizballah have appeared in the Carnegie Endowment's *Arab Reform Bulletin*, *Survival*, and *Small Wars and Insurgencies*. He is the author of *The Counterinsurgent State: Provincial Dissent and State-Formation in Iraq, 1919–1945*, forthcoming from Palgrave-MacMillan Press.

Charles Wolf, Jr.

Charles Wolf, Jr., is Senior Economic Adviser and Corporate Fellow in International Economics at RAND Corporation and a professor of public policy in the Pardee RAND Graduate School. From 1967 until 1981, he was head of RAND's Economics Department; thereafter, he was Director of RAND Research in International Economics. He was the founding dean of the RAND Graduate School and served in that capacity from 1970 to 1997.

Wolf received his B.S. and Ph.D. degrees in economics from Harvard. His main research and policy interests are the international economy, international security, and the relations between them. He is a Senior Research Fellow at the Hoover Institution, and a director of both Capital Income Builder Fund, Inc., and Capital World Growth and Income Fund, Inc. He has served with the U.S. Department of State and has taught at Cornell, University of California at Berkeley, UCLA, and Nuffield College, Oxford.

Wolf is the author of more than 250 journal articles and the author or co-author of two dozen books, including *Markets or Governments: Choosing Between Imperfect Alternatives,* MIT Press, 1993; *The Economic Pivot in a Political Context,* 1997; *Asian Economic Trends and Their Security Implications,* 2000 (available at http://www.rand.org/pubs/monograph_reports/MR1143/); *Straddling Economics and Politics: Cross-Cutting Issues in Asia, the United States, and the Global Economy,* 2002 (available at http://www.rand.org/pubs/monograph_reports/MR1571/); *Fault Lines in China's Economic Terrain,* 2003 (available at http://www.rand.org/pubs/monograph_reports/MR1686/); *North Korean Paradoxes: Circumstances, Costs, and Consequences of Korean Unification,* 2005 (available at http://www.rand.org/pubs/monographs/MG333/); *Russia's Economy: Signs of Progress and Retreat on the Transitional Road,* 2006 (available at http://www.rand.org/pubs/monographs/MG515/). He is a frequent contributor to *The Wall Street Journal, The Asian Wall Street Journal, The Wall Street Journal Europe, The New York Times,* and *The Los Angeles Times.*

References

Abdin, Mahan, "Public Opinion and the Nuclear Standoff," *Mideast Mirror*, Vol.1, No. 2, April/May 2006.

al-Gharib, Muhammad 'Abdallah, 1988. *Wa Ja'a Dur al-Majus* (And Then Came the Turn of the Magi). As of October 19, 2007:
http://www.tawhed.ws/a?i=402

al-Hasan, Bilal, 2007. "Ahmadinejad's Grave Mistake: The Theory of Vacuum Filling" (in Arabic), *Al Sharq Al Awsat*, September 2, 2007.

al-Saffar, Hassan, 2006. *Al-Madhhab wa al-Watan* (Sect and Homeland), Beirut: Arab Foundation for Studies and Publishing, 2006.

al-Saffar, Hassan, 2007. "La wa Lan Nuqbil Aya' Marja'n Takfiri'an wa Arfad Tadkhal aya' Marja' fi al-Shu'un al-Siyasiya al-Dakhiliya li-Biladna (We Do Not and Will Not Welcome Any Marja' [Spiritual Reference] That Promotes Takfir [Excommunication] and I Oppose the Interference of Any Marja' in the Internal Political Affairs of Our Country), *Al-Risala*, February 16, 2007.

al-Sayf, Tawfiq, 2002. *Nathariyat al-Sulta fi al-Fiqh al-Shi'i* (Theories of Political Power in Shiite Jurisprudence), Beirut: Center for Arabic Culture, 2002.

al-Zarqawi, Abu Musab, n.d.. *Hal Ataka Hadith al-Rawafidh?* (Has Word of the Rejectionists [Shiites] Reached You?), audio recording, n.d. As of October 15, 2007:
http://www.tawhed.ws/r?i=4048

Anon., 2006. "Tactless Mubarak Provokes Reassertion of National Loyalties by Gulf Arab Shias," *Gulf States Newsletter*, Vol. 30, Issue 779, April 14, 2006.

BBC Monitoring, 2007a. *Profile of Iran's New Nuclear Negotiator Jalili*, IAP20071025011006, Caversham, United Kingdom: *BBC Monitoring* in English, October 25, 2007.

———, 2007b. "Iranian 'Nuclear Spy' Row Flares Up Among Senior Leaders," FEA20071114408626, Open Source Center Feature, *BBC Monitoring*, November 13, 2007.

————, 2008. *Media Environment Guide: Iran*, IAP20080716011002, Caversham, United Kingdom: *BBC Monitoring* in English, July 16, 2008.

Bozorghmehr, Najmeh, 2006. "Nuclear Row Sparks Echoes of Iran's Brutal War with Iraq," *The Financial Times*, October 26, 2006, p. 5.

Chubin, Shahram, 2006. *Iran's Nuclear Ambitions*, Washington, D.C.: Carnegie Endowment for International Peace, September 2006.

————, 2007. "Iran: Domestic Politics and Nuclear Choices," in Michael Wills and Ashley Tellis, eds., *Strategic Asia 2007–08: Domestic Political Change and Grand Strategy*, Washington, D.C.: National Bureau of Asian Research (NBR), December 2007.

Chubin, Shahram, and Robert Litwak, 2003. "Debating Iran's Nuclear Aspirations," *The Washington Quarterly*, Autumn, 2003, pp. 104–107.

Gause, F. Gregory III, "Saudi Arabia: Iraq, Iran, the Regional Power Balance and the Sectarian Question," *Strategic Insights*, February 2007.

Geiling, Saskia, 1997. "The *Marja'iya* in Iran and the Nomination of Khamanei in December 1994," *Middle Eastern Studies,* 33:4, 1997, pp. 777–787.

Herzog, Michael, "Iranian Public Opinion on the Nuclear Program," *Policy Focus*, No. 56, Washington Institute, June 2006.

Jones, Toby Craig, 2007. "Saudi Arabia's Not So New Anti-Shiism," *Middle East Report*, No. 242, Spring 2007, pp. 29–32.

Kaye, Dalia Dassa, 2007. *Talking to the Enemy: Track Two Diplomacy in the Middle East and South Asia*, Santa Monica, Calif.: RAND Corporation, 2007. As of August 26, 2008:
http://www.rand.org/pubs/monographs/MG592/

Khalaj, Mehdi, "Ahmadinejad's Popularity One Year On," *Policy Watch*, No. 1125, Washington Institute, July 20, 2006.

Management and Planning Organization of Iran, 2007. Website. As of July 2007:
http://www.mporg.ir/ghanoon86/jadavel%20kalan/A02.html

Mathee, Rudee, 1986. "The Egyptian Opposition on the Iranian Revolution," in Juan R. I. Cole and Nikki R. Keddie, eds., *Shi'ism and Social Protest*, New Haven: Yale University Press, 1986, pp. 247–274.

Nafisi, Rasool, 2006. "The Khomeini Letter: Is Rafsanjani Warning the Hardliners?" Iranian.com, October 11, 2006. As of August 24, 2008:
http://www.iranian.com/RasoolNafisi/2006/October/Nuclear/index.html

National Intelligence Council, "Iran: Nuclear Intentions and Capabilities," National Intelligence Estimate, November 2007. As of August 26, 2008:
http://www.dni.gov/press_releases/20071203_release.pdf

Open Source Center, 2007. "FYI—Iran's Al-Alam TV Discusses Arab Reaction to Saddam's Execution," IAP20070102950094, Tehran, *Al-Alam* TV in Arabic, 1330 GMT, January 2, 2007.

Sadjadpour, Karim, 2008. *Reading Khamenei: The World View of Iran's Most Powerful Leader*, Washington, D.C.: Carnegie Endowment for International Peace, March 2008. As of March 17, 2008:
http://www.carnegieendowment.org/publications/index.cfm?fa=view&id=19975

United States Government Accounting Office, 2007. *Report to the Ranking Member, Subcommittee on National Security and Foreign Affairs, House Committee on Oversight and Government Reform. IRAN SANCTIONS: Impact in Furthering U.S. Objectives Is Unclear and Should Be Reviewed*, December 2007. As of August 20, 2008:
http://www.gao.gov/new.items/d0858.pdf

Valbjørn, Morten, and André Bank, 2007. "Signs of a New Arab Cold War: The 2006 Lebanon War and the Sunni-Shi'i Divide," *Middle East Report*, Spring 2007.

Wehrey, Fred, 2007. "Saudi Arabia: Shi'a Pessimistic About Reform, but Seek Reconciliation," *Arab Reform Bulletin*, Vol. 5, Issue 5, June 2007. As of August 26, 2008:
http://www.carnegieendowment.org/publications/index.cfm?fa=view&id=19217#wehrey

World Public Opinion, 2007. *Public Opinion in Iran and America on International Issues*, report on a WorldPublicOpinion.org poll conducted in partnership with Search for Common Grond and Knowledge Networks, January 24, 2007. As of September 25, 2008:
http://www.worldpublicopinion.org/pipa/articles/brmiddleeastnafricara/311.php?nid=&id=&pnt=311

Zogby International, "Inside Iran—Exclusive Reader's Digest/Zogby International Poll of Iranians Reveals a Society in Flux," July 13, 2006. As of September 25, 2008:
http://www.zogby.com/news/ReadNews.dbm?ID=1147

Zonis, Marvin, 1971. *The Political Elite of Iran*, Princeton, N.J.: Princeton University Press, 1971.